Nicola Slee is Research Fellow and M
Queen's Foundation for Ecumenical Theol
UK. She also works freelance, doing a v
ing and retreat work, with a particular commitment to researching
and supporting the spirituality and faith development of women and
girls. Her recent publications include *The Book of Mary* (SPCK, 2007),
The Edge of God (co-edited with Michael N. Jagessar and Stephen
Burns, Epworth, 2008) and *Presiding Like a Woman* (co-edited with
Stephen Burns, SPCK, 2010). She lives in Stirchley, Birmingham, with
her partner and their two cats.

SEEKING THE RISEN CHRISTA

NICOLA SLEE

First published in Great Britain in 2011

Society for Promoting Christian Knowledge
36 Causton Street
London SW1P 4ST
www.spckpublishing.co.uk

British Library Cataloguing-in-Publication Data
A catalogue record for this book is available from the British Library

ISBN 978–0–281–06256–0

1 3 5 7 9 10 8 6 4 2

Typeset by Graphicraft Ltd, Hong Kong
Printed in Great Britain by Ashford Colour Press

Produced on paper from sustainable forests

For Rosie

Contents

Preface

This book would have been inconceivable without the pioneering work of feminist theologians and contemporary artists (reviewed in Chapter 1), who have envisaged and realized a female Christ figure, and I gladly acknowledge the generativity of their work for my own. However, the seed of the book owes its genesis more particularly to a shared women's Easter retreat I helped to facilitate in 2006 (described in more detail in Chapter 1), at Noddfa, Penmaenmawr, when the question 'where is the risen Christa?' first began to formulate itself. I would like to thank all the women who took part in that week for the creativity of our time together and the sisters who run the retreat centre at Noddfa for their warm hospitality and the freedom they blessed us with to do our own thing. Pat Pierce, one of the women who shared the leadership of that time with me (and who painted an enormous image of the Christa during the retreat), has been an inspiration over many years: clear-sighted, courageous and free-thinking, she is a risen woman in whom I recognize the face of the Christa.

The idea for the book emerged out of that time and grew slowly over the next few years. A three-month sabbatical granted by the governors of the Queen's Foundation in summer 2009 gave me the space I needed to focus on the project, and I am grateful to both staff and governors of Queen's who made it possible for me to take this time out from my normal duties. I was fortunate enough to be awarded a research scholarship at Vaughan Park Anglican Retreat Centre, Long Bay, one of the lovely beach suburbs of Auckland. I owe a very special debt to all the staff at Vaughan Park, and most particularly to John Fairbrother, the Director, and his wife Margaret, for their generous Kiwi hospitality. Vaughan Park is not only a beautiful place to set down for a while, with the beach and parkland right on one's doorstep, but a place of wide and inclusive welcome, of liberality of mind and heart, of authentic and lived spirituality. I found it a place of welcome, renewal, healing and vitality, where I was encouraged to relish my freedom and inhabit the space in whatever way was good for me. I was nourished and held by a rhythm of daily prayer and regular eucharistic worship from the New Zealand Prayer Book (still unsurpassed in the Anglican Communion for its creativity and inclusivity), as well as by excellent food and free-flowing New Zealand wines, and above all, by the loving friendship I received from the community. I enjoyed many stimulating conversations about the project – and much more besides – with John and Margaret and others, and had a number of opportunities for trying out some of the poems in this book with the worshipping community.

There have been other opportunities to share some of the ideas in the book, and I am grateful for a number of invitations to do so. As any poet knows, one really has to hear a poem aloud, preferably in a gathered group of attentive listeners, to receive it oneself. The two small writing groups to which I belong, a local one in Birmingham and a more dispersed group, have both heard many Christa poems over the past few years, and have followed the development of Christa's exploits with interest, offering me encouragement as well as attentive, constructive criticism. The members of both groups have all become, if they weren't already, good friends, and people whose wisdom, not only with words, I rely upon. My gratitude to Gavin D'Costa, Eleanor Nesbitt and Ruth Shelton, of the Diviners (as we call ourselves) and to Penny Hewlett, Rosie Miles and Sibyl Ruth of the Edge group. Other larger and more formal groups graciously heard my Christa offerings at various stages and made thoughtful and intelligent responses. I am grateful for opportunities to give lectures on the ideas in the book at Vaughan Park, towards the end of my time there; at the United Theological College, Parramatta, Sydney (by kind invitation of Stephen Burns); at the Centre for Radical Christianity, St Mark's, Sheffield (at the invitation of Ian Wallis, an old friend and colleague from Aston Training Scheme days) and at Greenbelt 2010. I also shared early versions of some of the material in the book with the Women and Religion seminar and with various of my feminist theology classes at Queen's.

Lecturing about the Christa is one thing; reading poems about her another; preaching and praying the Christa, in the context of a gathered Christian community, is something else again. I had the awesome privilege of being invited by Charles Hedley to give the addresses at the Good Friday Three Hours at St James, Piccadilly, in 2010 and, in close consultation with Lindsay Meader and others, decided to focus the liturgy on the Christa. I can't think of another

Anglican church in the UK that would have welcomed the Christa in the way that folks at St James did, showing themselves willing to be challenged and stretched to reflect on the suffering of Christ in new forms and symbols. I am hugely grateful to the clergy and people of St James for that opportunity and for their prayerful and lively response to the Christa.

Particular individuals have inspired various of the poems in the book, and they are acknowledged in the notes at the back and sometimes named in the poems themselves. There are a number of others who have encouraged this book, and me in the writing of it, to whom I owe much. Ruth McCurry, my editor at SPCK, has been an advocate of my work over several years now, and continues to offer a characteristic mixture of affirmation and pragmatic wisdom that comes out of years of publishing experience as well as her own passionate commitment to women's full participation in the Church. Lauren Zimmerman steered the manuscript through to the copy-editing process with efficiency and helpful advice, and Jennifer Wild undertook the copy-editing with a sharp eye for detail and a broader understanding of what I am attempting to do in this work.

Three individuals read the manuscript closely and gave me helpful feedback. Al Barrett trained for ordained ministry at Queen's back in the late nineties, and is a very fine parish priest in the Birmingham diocese and a theologian of considerable creativity. He offered me particular encouragement to believe that this book has a real contribution to make to ordinary parish ministry. I wish I could have taken up some of his suggestions for including illustrations of the Christa in the book (this would have been too costly and time-consuming) and for offering practical guidance about how to use the book in a parish setting (the idea came too late in the day to be incorporated). I look to Al to do some of that work of application and to share it with me – and others.

I first met Stephen Burns when he came to work at Queen's in 2002. We have worked together now on a number of writing projects and, over the years, Stephen has not only been a stimulating colleague but has become a much valued and most generous friend. He has accompanied me in this writing venture from start to finish, pointing me in the direction of visual images of the Christa, offering me ideas and sources I might not otherwise have come across and, most of all, helping me interpret my own work to myself through many email conversations, in which he has drawn on his prodigious knowledge of contemporary theology to set my modest efforts within a wider context of current theological trends and debates and see how it might contribute to these. As a fine liturgist, Stephen has not only understood but actively shared in my quest for a feminist language of prayer, encouraging me to take the Christa – or recognize her – at the heart of the public prayer of the Church. This book would not have made it into the light of day without Stephen's encouragement and support, and I am hugely grateful for both.

My partner, Rosie Miles, knows more than anyone what this book means to me, and the journey out of which it has come. She has encouraged me to believe in its significance for others, both known and unknown, for whom and with whom I have written it – of whom she is the foremost. If my own writing has flourished in the past ten years and brought me to a point of conceiving and birthing this book, that is in no small measure due to what I receive from our shared life: a rootedness and a freedom born from a profound knowledge of being loved that enables me to give myself deeply to my own work, to take risks I might not otherwise take and to fly freely where I might not have dared venture. My every book's first reader, this one is dedicated very particularly to Rosie in her own journey towards risenness.

And then there are the cats. Affectionately referred to in our household as 'the face of the divine', neither Tinker nor Pumpkin appear to strive to realize their incarnate beauty or joyous risenness. They grace us with their feline presences, which weave in and out of our days. If Christa has her own familiars – and surely she does – they are creatures such as these.

Nicola Slee
Stirchley

1

Seeking the risen Christa

Introduction

Questions in search of the risen Christa

Why is the Christa always suffering, broken, dying?
Where is the risen Christa?
Why have we not realized her?
Is she still on her way to us?
How can we help her arrive?

When she comes to us, will we know her?
Will her face be turned towards us
or looking away, beyond our stifled horizons?

Will her eyes be filled with compassion or fury?
Will we dare to meet her gaze?

How will she greet us?
Will she touch us, or shake us?
What will she say to us?
Will we recognize the sound of her voice speaking?
Or will she approach through torrential silences?

Where shall we go looking for her?
Who will show us her way?

Seeking a risen Christa

Questions around the identity and significance of Jesus the Christ are not merely academic ones, but touch to the heart of lived faith. Whatever else we might want to say about Christianity, the centrality of Jesus the Christ to our faith cannot be doubted. Christians believe different things about Jesus, argue about who he was and what he was about, and disagree about the best doctrinal formulations to express Christian belief in Christ. Some emphasize that Christianity is, first and foremost, a walking in the way of Jesus rather than a holding to certain (later) beliefs about him. Others assert the primacy of the classic conciliar proclamations about Christ, as contained in the creeds, as non-negotiable and central to faith.

In my own Christian discipleship, the person and the way of Christ have been central from the start, yet the ways in which I have expressed my understanding of Jesus, and the forms my devotion to Jesus has taken, have changed quite dramatically over some four decades. Though blissfully unaware of doubts and misgivings in my early Christian journey, increasingly I have wrestled with what it can mean, not only to *think* or *image* Christ in authentic ways, but what it can mean for a feminist woman who does not wish to be in disempowering or inauthentic relation to any male Other, to be in relation to Christ within the community of those who seek to follow in the way of Jesus and live according to his teaching. Growing up in a low-church Methodist tradition and experiencing the liveliness of faith as a teenager in evangelical circles, the person of Jesus was absolutely central to my sense of faith and of God. My prayer life, my reading of Scripture and my sense of myself as saved and loved by God were all rooted in an intensely personal, quasi-erotic relationship with Jesus – a relationship I now look back on with a mixture of gratitude and embarrassment. Gratitude, because Jesus truly mirrored and incarnated to me the overwhelming and costly love of God, and still does; embarrassment, because I now see how uncritically my spiritualized notion of Jesus and my privatized relationship with him mirrored some of the worst features of a white middle-class patriarchal upbringing, unthinkingly absorbed. My Jesus was made in the image of the ideal man I hoped to meet and marry: intelligent, sensitive, passionate, empathic, discerning, generous, utterly dependable and offering me a belief in myself and my worth that I did not, then, possess.[1]

In time, such a model of Jesus gradually self-destructed, partly through my theological education, especially through my encounters with feminist theology; and partly through my own psychological struggles and growing. I discovered that my Jesus did not save me from the pains and confusions of family breakdown, academic failure, disappointment in love or fear of the future. Jesus was no nice husband substitute, protecting me from the challenges of life. I needed to get real and grow up, and in the process let go the clinging, cloying love-relationship to a spiritualized heterosexual lover that Jesus represented. The story of Mary Magdalene loving and losing her relationship with the earthly Jesus, as read by Elisabeth Moltmann-Wendel and others, came to mean much to me.[2] As the Magdalene had to stop clinging to her beloved Jesus and leave the garden of intimate encounter in order to discover a wider, freer Christ – so did I.[3]

This book – a series of poems, prayers and reflections on the Christa – is a continuation, then, of a lifelong journey of theological and spiritual quest for the incarnate, dying and risen one who mediates to human beings the face and the grace of God. To some readers, especially those versed in contemporary feminist theology, the idea of the Christa will not be new, having been debated and imaged by many feminist theologians and artists over the past three decades or so. However, for the majority of readers, I suspect the very notion of the Christa will be startlingly, perhaps disconcertingly, new. So it is important, in this introduction, to take some time to trace the history of the emergence of the idea of the Christa in recent feminist thought, to explain why this figure has emerged and what some of its meanings might be – but also, as I hope, to demonstrate that this is an idea or image which has a long and ancient past, rooted in Christian tradition, prayer and spirituality, including the Scriptures and classic Christology. Thus, while some see any attempt to image Christ in female form as outrageous, even blasphemous, I shall argue that, rightly understood, the Christa is entirely compatible with orthodox Christian faith (though this is not to say that all theologians who advocate the Christa conform to one pattern of faith), and is simply one of a myriad ways of incarnating and re-imaging the humanity and divinity of Christ so that contemporary believers – especially but not only women – may appropriate the Christian gospel anew.

In what follows, I shall first attempt briefly to set a context for the emergence of the figure of the Christa in contemporary feminist theology but also in the wider postmodern religious scene, before going on to chart in some detail the emergence of the Christa in feminist theology and art, considering some of the key representations of a female Christ by artists and exploring the range of meanings which feminist theologians bring to the Christa. Unfortunately, it has not been possible to include reproductions of the many Christa images to which I shall refer, but in most cases these are available on the web, and I shall provide full details of sources in the notes. Having begun in the present, I shall then look backwards over the history of Christian tradition to demonstrate that the idea of a female Christ is nothing new, but a very ancient idea rooted in Scripture, tradition and Christian practice down the centuries. This overview of the historical roots of the Christa cannot hope to be comprehensive or systematic, but I hope to do enough to counter any claims that the idea is a purely modern invention of feminists. Nothing, in fact, can be further from the truth – even if contemporary feminists have taken the tradition further, and fleshed it out, in ways that are startling and fresh. Finally, and returning to the project of this book, I shall outline my own journey of developing interest in the Christa, and narrate the origins of the book in a shared women's Easter retreat a few years ago, before offering a brief overview of the book as a whole and inviting readers to share with me the journey in search of a risen Christa.

Setting a context for the Christa

The first and most obvious context within which interest in the Christa has emerged is the context of feminist theology, and in particular, feminist Christology. Feminist theologians have been debating the person of Jesus and Christian claims about the Christ for decades now, and there is a vast literature from around the globe testifying to a lively diversity of feminist Christologies.[4] Debate has centred on a wide range of issues: questions around the historical Jesus and his attitudes towards, teaching about, and relationships with women; issues around the significance of Jesus' gender and the symbolism of a male saviour, especially whether this reinforces or, in various ways, challenges and subverts patriarchy; questions about the cross and atonement theory and whether there are constructive ways of understanding both that are liberating for women (and men); explorations of traditional Trinitarian theologies and the place of Christ within the Trinity; exegeses of various themes within the teaching and praxis of Jesus, particularly around his teaching of the kingdom (*basileia*) – or kin-dom – of God, his practice of table fellowship and his inclusive friendships with many considered marginal in the mainstream religious and political cultures of his day.

These and many other themes have been explored in feminist Christologies. While post-Christians such as Mary Daly, Naomi Goldenberg and Daphne Hampson conclude that there is no possibility of redeeming Christology and that the notion of a male saviour must be abandoned,[5] Christian feminists offer a wide range of positive proposals for rethinking classical Christology, including regendering models of Christ, rethinking the relationship between the Jesus of history and the Christ of faith, decentring the significance of Jesus or Christ within a wider understanding of God or Trinity, and a variety of other possible positions. Within the breadth of feminist Christological discourse, the figure of the female Christ, or the Christa, is a particularly potent image – representing one, but only one, means of refiguring, reassembling Christology. This figure provides the focus of this book, although I do not believe it is the *only* way of representing Christ. No one model or image, however creative or rich, can hope to hold all the shifting significance and meanings we might want to discern in the Christ. I want to explore the image and the concept of Christa, at the same time as holding open other ways of thinking about Jesus and other names for Christ.

While feminist reflection on Jesus is the most obvious context in which the Christa has emerged, I would suggest that we need to look wider in order to discern the significance of this new expression of Christology. Feminist theology, itself, can be seen as one among a number of liberation movements emerging from the repressed underside of patriarchal religion (along with black theology, post-colonial theology, gay, lesbian and queer theologies, and so on), which are both critiquing and renewing religion in radical and subversive ways. Each of these liberation movements points to the oppressive nature of religion in a variety of respects, and yet, at the same time, offers hope of renewing religion at its roots as that which has been denied, marginalized and repressed is taken back into the mainstream and enabled to heal the splits which have rent asunder the Christian tradition and the body of Christ. Liberation theology is restoring the huge spiritual and political resources of the poor to the centre of Christianity, black and post-colonial theology is returning the experience of millions of black and Asian people to the tradition, feminist theology is enabling the forgotten faith of half the human race to find its place once again at the heart of the mainstream, and gay, lesbian and queer theologies are asserting the positive value of the experience of repressed sexual minorities to our understanding of faith. In these and many other ways, liberation theology movements are both disrupting what has come to be taken for granted for millennia within the Christian mainstream and offering restoration, renewal and rehabilitation. Thus feminist and other liberation theologies can be seen to signal a wide-ranging crisis within institutional religions about the meaning and relevance of their stories, symbols and practices and the very viability of religion in the twenty-first century, even as such theologies represent creative responses to this crisis. The Christa is one example, though certainly not the only one, of a traditional religious symbol – the symbol of Christ – in crisis, in transition, in deconstruction; a symbol that is being radically questioned, critiqued, playfully parodied and imaginatively represented. While some find this a fearful and threatening prospect, undermining the stability of the tradition, others recognize and grasp with open arms the potential of such a process for revivifying and renewing the symbols and stories that are in danger of ossifying and becoming moribund.

So, I want to say, the Christa is not some minority, off-beam, idiosyncratic preoccupation of a group of specialist academics or extreme feminists – or, if it is, it nevertheless has a far greater and wider significance, beyond the confines of those who are actively preoccupied with the concept. The Christa is a signal to the wider Christian body of the creative crisis in which religion finds itself, and it is a signal of the neglected and repressed resources which Christianity has within itself to respond to such a crisis. To put this another way, the Christa is one among many symbols of a re-emergence of the (divine) feminine, both within Christianity and other faith traditions, but also outside mainstream religions, which is part of a universal movement of repressed peoples and paths finding their voices and insisting on their experience, wisdom and gifts being recognized and taken seriously. Christianity rejects that wisdom and those gifts at its peril, expelling the very life force that can heal and revivify the ancient paths.

The Christa in contemporary feminist theology and art

'As women have been told they do not resemble the saviour, we are in the process of "reassembling" that figure.'[6]

The figure of the female Christ or the Christa has been a recurring motif in Christian feminist theological writings since the 1970s, provoked by the creation of a sculpture of that name by Edwina Sandys in 1974 for the United Nations Decade for Women: Equality, Development and Peace (1976–1985).[7] The sculpture – a nude female form wearing a crown of thorns with arms outstretched in the form of a crucified figure – was displayed in the Cathedral of St John the Divine, New York, during Holy Week, 1984, and caused something of an uproar, eliciting strongly divided reactions from those who viewed it. A second sculpture, *Crucified Woman*, made by a German-born Canadian sculptor, Almuth Lutkenhause-Lackey, in the same year, 1974,[8] was displayed in the chancel of Bloor Street United Church, Toronto, during Lent, Holy Week and Eastertide 1979 – and again, the image caused controversy. Lutkenhause-Lackey subsequently offered the work as a gift to Emmanuel College, Toronto, and the work was installed in the grounds in 1986.

While these two works are probably the best known of the so-called Christa figures, there are multiple forms of the crucified or cruciform woman in art, literature and film, as well as in feminist theology. A search on Google for images of crucified women will yield a surprising number of such forms (some being of serious theological intent, some playful or parodic and others of a fairly dubious semi-pornographic nature). Julie Clague has reviewed some representations of the Christa, highlighting in particular *Crucifixion, Shoalhaven* by Arthur Boyd (1979–80), *Christine on the Cross* by James M. Murphy (1984) and *Bosnian Christa* by Margaret Argyll (1993)[9] – but there are others. Kittredge Cherry has brought together a range of images of the female Christ, alongside those of a gay Jesus, in her book, *Art That Dares: Gay Jesus, Woman Christ, and More.*[10] Jill Ansell, Robert

Lentz, Janet McKenzie, William McHart Nichols and Sandra Yagi have each created novel and striking images of the female Christ.[11] As well as paintings and sculptures, a number of photographic images of the Christa figure have appeared recently, including reworkings of the Last Supper depicting a female Christ and female disciples[12] and more examples of the crucified female Christ,[13] as well as film and video versions.[14]

Feminist theologians have taken up the suggestive notion of the Christa and developed it in a range of ways. In her classic *Sexism and God-Talk*, Rosemary Radford Ruether proposes the notion of Christ in female form (though she does not use the Christa title). She calls attention to the way in which the Christian community continues Christ's identity and presence in the world today, and since this community includes women, it is perfectly legitimate, even necessary, for women to therefore represent Christ. 'In the language of early Christian prophetism, we can encounter Christ *in the form of our sister.* Christ, the liberated humanity, is not confined to a static perfection of one person two thousand years ago.'[15]

Carter Heyward similarly makes a distinction between the Jesus of history – 'a Jewish male with a particular relationship to his "abba"' – and Christ, who 'may be for Christians the salvific implications of the Jesus story' or 'the characterization of justice-making with compassion, courage, and integrity'.[16] Rather than focusing on the historical Jesus, she wants to speak of what can be and is 'christic', in other words Christ-forming or Christ-making, in our common experience and search for justice – and for Heyward, this is always allied to the search for and creation of right relations, both in the interpersonal sphere but also more widely in society at large:

> Whatever/whoever may be christic for us will emerge in the contemporary crossroads of religious/spiritual pluralism, global movements for liberation from oppression, a feminist commitment to justice for women and to making connections between the liberation of women and of all who suffer injustice, and commitments to a sane and respectful relation to the earth and its varied creatures.[17]

This enables Heyward to speak of Christ or Christa in female, as well as male, terms – not as something external to us, but as a way of speaking about our collective responsibility for and commitment to right relation in the world. Thus Heyward speaks of believers and justice-seekers as those who are both the bearers and the fulfilment of the vision of 'the common-wealth of joy': 'both *theotokos*, the bearer, and *corpus christa*, the born'. She continues:

> We know that together, in solidarity, we are she: women and men, older and younger, people of different races and cultures and religions, we are she. Lesbians and gaymen, heterosexual men and women, married and single, with our diverse gifts and our divergent interests, in our shared commitment to human well-being, we are she. In our own Christian faith we know that in our shared commitment to human well-being, we are she: bearer and born, mother and child. We are the Christa.[18]

Rita Nakashima Brock develops Heyward's relational, justice-seeking approach in her *Journeys by Heart: A Christology of Erotic Power*, a book that has had a significant impact on the development of the notion of the Christa in feminist Christology. Like Ruether and Heyward, Brock argues that feminist Christology must not be centred in the historic figure of Jesus, however much it may draw on the inspiration and teachings of Jesus, because that is to make of one individual, and a male at that, a heroic saviour figure to whom women look for meaning and guidance, thus reinforcing what Mary Daly earlier described as 'Christolatry',[19] an unhealthy idolization of Jesus that disempowers women and prevents us from claiming our own spiritual authority.

Drawing on Audre Lorde's classic essay on the erotic[20] and Susan Griffin's work on erotic power,[21] as well as on the poems of Adrienne Rich,[22] Nakashima Brock develops a Christology of erotic power, in which Christ becomes a symbol of the fundamental power of existence which is seen as a dynamic, erotic energy of relational process. Her Christology, rather than being centred in Jesus, is centred 'in relationship and community as the whole-making, healing center of Christianity', a reality she names 'Christa/Community'. 'In using Christa instead of Christ', she writes, 'I am using a term that points away from sole identification of Christ with Jesus. In combining it with community, I want to shift the focus of salvation away from heroic individuals, male or female.'[23]

> Jesus participates centrally in this Christa/Community, but he neither brings erotic power into being nor controls it. He is brought into being through it and participates in the cocreation of it. Christa/Community

is a lived reality expressed in relational images. Hence Christa/Community is described in the images of events in which erotic power is made manifest. The reality of erotic power within connectedness means it cannot be located in a single individual. Hence what is truly Christological, that is, truly revealing of divine incarnation and salvific power in human life, must reside in connectedness and not in single individuals.[24]

Nakashima Brock offers a reading of the Gospel of Mark in which this erotic power is seen at work, particularly in Jesus' exorcisms and healings, and in the Passion narrative. The exorcisms are symbols of liberation from internalized oppression while the healing stories show what happens in social relationships when hierarchical powers are removed. Moreover, the focus is not so much on Jesus per se as on the community that included Jesus. Jesus alone does not possess erotic power, but this power is revealed and expressed when members of the community are connected and the power is able to flow through the connections. Erotic power also flows through the Passion narrative – again, not so much localized in the suffering or the body of Jesus, as in the wider Christa community. The incompleteness of Mark's Gospel – ending abruptly with the women leaving the empty tomb in fear – along with the significant presence of women throughout the Passion narrative acting in ways that affirm divine presence, both point to the ongoing 'Christa/Community that would survive Jesus' death and witness his resurrection'.[25]

Ultimately, according to Nakashima Brock's reading of Mark, the gospel calls us to a communal claiming of the presence and erotic power of Christ in the Christa/Community:

> The resurrection of Jesus is a powerful image of the need for solidarity among and with victims of oppressive powers. The resurrection affirms that no one person alone can overcome brokenness. Each of us lives in each other in Christa/Community. In caring for each other and in passionately affirming erotic power, we struggle on our journey to create spaces for it to flourish. In standing in solidarity with all who suffer, we must be willing to confront and feel deeply the tragic loss of all who suffer and die and to be empowered to act, even when afraid. Guided by heart, we must travel with each other and remember all who have gone before. By embracing and healing heart, our willingness not to allow brokenheartedness to continue sets us on the way of erotic power.[26]

While I have not been able to find any instances of black, womanist or Asian women theologians speaking of the Christa as such, the notion of a female Christ figure is certainly not strange to them. Womanist theologians such as Jacquelyn Grant and Kelly Douglas Brown draw on a long tradition of black women's struggle for liberation, in which they see the face of the Christ imaged, as well as on the work of multiple black male theologians who have asserted that Christ is black.[27]

Perhaps the most striking and powerful rendering of a black Christa comes from the famous speech of the nineteenth-century anti-slave campaigner, Sojourner Truth. Born a slave in the late 1700s in upstate New York, Sojourner Truth laboured for a succession of five masters until slavery was officially abolished on 4 July 1827, and then became an itinerant preacher and was a popular and powerful speaker at abolitionist and women's rights events. Her 'Ain't I a woman' speech, delivered at a woman's rights convention in Akron, Ohio, 1851, has taken on a kind of iconic status in womanist thought in general and womanist theology in particular, for its authoritative witness to black women's suffering and oppression, but also for its assertion of a profound theology rooted in the slave women's experience. Responding to earlier speakers who had made much of the maleness of Christ as a reason for limiting women's rights and who had appealed to women's need for male protection, Truth challenged such arguments in her speech:

> That man over there says that women need to be helped into carriages and lifted over ditches, and to have the best place everywhere. Nobody ever helps me into carriages, or over mud-puddles, or gives me any best place! And ain't I a woman? Look at me! Look at my arm! I could have ploughed and planted, and gathered into barns, and no man could head me! And ain't I a woman? I could work as much and eat as much as a man – when I could get it – and bear the lash as well! And ain't I a woman? I have borne thirteen children, and seen them most all sold off to slavery, and when I cried out with my mother's grief, none but Jesus heard me! And ain't I a woman? . . .
>
> Then that little man in black there, he says women can't have as much rights as men, 'cause Christ wasn't a woman! Where did your Christ come from? From God and a woman! Man had nothing to do with Him.[28]

This speech by an illiterate, uneducated former slave is remarkable for its implicit Christology, offering a rich, many-textured theology of the Christa. Here we see a Christ in solidarity with the sufferings of black women ('none but Jesus heard me'), a Christ whose origins have 'nothing to do with' male power, privilege or status, whose being is rooted in the being of God and the being of woman – who is the source and the power of black women's, and all women's, liberation. And in her own fearless truthfulness and risen courage, Sojourner Truth herself can rightfully be regarded as a type of the Christa herself.

Building on the liberation struggles and faith of women like Sojourner Truth, Harriet Tubman and Fannie Lou Hamer, contemporary womanist theologians such as Grant and Brown Douglas challenge the dominance of black male images of Christ in male black theology, and assert that 'Christ, found in the experience of Black women, is a Black woman'.[29] Kelly Brown Douglas speaks of a 'womanist Black Christ' which will 'avail itself of a diversity of symbols and icons', not to be confined exclusively or unthinkingly to female representations but nevertheless working consistently to 'lift up the presence of Christ in the faces of the poorest Black women'.[30] Douglas reflects on the impact of her grandmother's faith in Christ on her own theology, and images Christ in the face of her grandmother:

> As I now reflect on my grandmother's faith in Christ, I realize that the Christ in her life had to be one who understood more than just what it meant to live in a racist society. My grandmother's Christ was one whom she could talk to about the daily struggles of being poor, Black, and female. So, it is in this regard that I continue to learn from my grandmother's faith. Her faith in Christ's empowering presence suggests, at the very least, a womanist Black Christ. But most importantly, it is in the face of my grandmother, as she struggled to sustain herself and her family, that I can truly see Christ.[31]

In a similarly experiential way, the Indian theologian Israel Selvanayagam remembers the way in which, in the poor household where he grew up, his mother would often share with him the last scraps of a meal she had cooked, and how this to him was a sacramental sharing:

> I grew up in the midst of grinding poverty. It was every time a challenge for my mother to work out a fair share among the hungry children and her husband. After eating my share, as the youngest in the family, I always waited to have a little from my mother's hand. It was very little and because she mixed the rice with the sticking bits of the fish curry mud-pan, sometimes with deep sighs, it was so special and so tasty. It was for me no less sacred than sharing a tiny piece of bread and a few drops of wine in a Communion.

The mother figure here is surely a Christa figure, sacrificially feeding her child not only with the tiny scraps of the meal, but perhaps more significantly with her bodily closeness, warmth and love. Selvanayagam goes on:

> Whenever I see babies suckling from the breast of their mothers I in my mind travel back to the upper room where Jesus and his disciples met for their last supper. Here there is a feeding with feet-washing, stroking, cuddling and at times shedding tears![32]

We are offered here an earthy and intimate image of the Christa who is both mother and priest, teacher and nurturer, feeder and food, washer and lover. (In line with Selvanayagam's eucharistic reflections, we might note here, in passing, that a number of feminist theologians and liturgists have recently explored the liturgical implications of the woman priest as an icon or image of the Christa, challenging more conservative notions of the [male] priest as an icon of the [male] Christ which exclude women from presiding at the eucharistic table.[33])

In her ground-breaking work on Asian women's theology, *Struggle to Be the Sun Again*, Chung Hyun Kyung alerts readers to the presence of a rich Asian women's Christology which draws on female images and icons to image Christ in an Asian context.[34] A number of Asian women depict Jesus as mother, woman and shaman. For example, Kwok Pui-lan, Lee Oo Chung and Marianne Katoppo each speak of Jesus as a compassionate, sensitive and pain-bearing mother, drawing on experiences and examples from their own Asian contexts.[35] Park Soon Kyung speaks of 'Jesus the *woman Messiah*' who is liberator of the oppressed,[36] and Choi Man Ja identifies Korean women's struggle for liberation with 'the praxis of messiahship', claiming that 'women are the true praxis of messiah-Jesus, in Korea'.[37] Perhaps most strikingly, Virginia Fabella and others speak of Jesus as the shaman who exorcises accumulated *han* – unexpressed anger and resentment resulting from social powerlessness – and heals and comforts the dispossessed.[38] Since in Korea the majority of shamans are women, to speak of Christ as a shaman is an Asian version of the Christa.

If feminist theology has developed the notion of the female Christ, and womanist and Asian theologies the notion of the black female Christ, queer and 'indecent' theologies have pushed the boundaries of this idea in more transgressive and deliberately subversive, playful, ways. Marcella Althaus-Reid warns of the dangers of feminist theology becoming settled and safe, a new kind of orthodoxy, against which her own brand of 'Indecent Theology' is a perpetual protest. She speaks of an 'obscene Christ',[39] drawing on Sartre's notion of the obscene as 'that which renders visible the flesh as flesh' and images Christ not only as female but as a poor female, as prostitute, as leather-clad lesbian, dying next to her lover, as the Bi/Christ who is neither male nor female, straight nor gay, beyond 'either this or that' 'because there are so many sexual identities to which we do not have names to give'.[40] Historically, she suggests, 'obscene Christs have appeared when people wanted to uncover the graceful pretences of current Christologies'. Thus, the black Christ was obscene because it uncovered white racism in Christology. Similarly, the Christa is obscene because 'it undresses the masculinity of God and produces feelings and questionings which were suppressed by centuries of identificatory masculine processes with God'.[41] Precisely by the visceral reactions which the viewer makes to a female crucified figure, deep cultural prejudices and attitudes to gender and sexuality are made visible for what they are. So Althaus-Reid asks,

> Why, for instance, is the tortured male body of Christ less offensive and infinitely more divine than a woman's tortured body? . . . Why is it that, confronted by the naked body of a female Christ, the hetero-sexual gaze is still fixed on the shape of breasts, the youth of the body and its sexual desirability?[42]

As Althaus-Reid's 'obscene Christ' is an attempt to destabilize and disrupt our assumptions about human sexuality and gender, simi-larly, Lisa Isherwood has developed the notion of the Fat Jesus[43] as a way of drawing attention to the hatred and fear of female flesh which is manifested in heteropatriarchy, particularly towards larger, older women. She challenges the idolization of thinness in Western, postmodern cultures, exposing the gendered symbolism of the ema-ciated, quasi-anorexic and youthful female form which can be read at one and the same time as an internalization, in the bodies of young women, of male fear and hatred of female flesh, and as a protest against it. In heteropatriarchy, she argues, women are alienated from their bodies and their deepest desires, and this can manifest in both under-eating, the self-starvation of the anorexic, and in over-eating, the rebellion of women who refuse to conform to the ideal of feminine beauty and dare to claim their own desires. In a society in which women are groomed from an early age to be the nurturers of others and to be desired by the other, 'women need to transform the need to be desired into an acceptance of desiring.'[44] The fat woman is the woman who dares to defy patriarchal ideals of feminine beauty, size and appetite, who manifests her own large desires in her own body, who takes up as much space in the world as she needs and wants – thus incurring the hatred and punishment of society. Our Christologies, she argues, both mirror and create the social and symbolic worlds we inhabit, and so she is in search of 'a Christ of womanly abundance', an 'erotic Christ' who is 'fully embodied, sensuous and seeking vulnerable commitment, alive with expectancy and power', a Christ who 'enables women to find their subjectivity and power' and 'live more fully in their skins'.[45] Although Isherwood never explicitly speaks of this fat Jesus as a fat *Christa*, nevertheless, it is clear that the fat Jesus is predicated on the celebration of fat women's bodies, sexualities and desires, and so she can speak of the fat Christ as 'she': 'We need the abject fat Jesus who bulges out all over the edges and carrie[s] her embodiment proudly and differently in the world.'[46]

Reactions to the Christa

Both the image and the concept of the Christa have caused controversy wherever they have been expressed – far in excess of comparable instances of, say, the black Christ, the Asian Christ or the Maori Christ. Whereas it appears to be acceptable to re-present Christ in a variety of ethnic and cultural forms, the notion of a female Christ – as, too, the notion of a gay Christ or the disabled Christ – is regarded by many as 'going too far', a denial of the historical particularity of Jesus' maleness, a fracturing of the symbolic significance of the crucifixion or even, by some, as blasphemous. Thus Bishop Walter D. Dennis, Suffragan of New York at the time of the exhibition of Edwina Sandys' *Christa*, described the sculpture as 'symbolically reprehensible' and 'theologically and historically indefensible'.[47] It is not only arch-conservatives and literalists who reject the symbolism of the female Christ. Feminists themselves are divided in their reactions to the Christa figure, with a number of feminists objecting to what they see as an image which assumes the male gaze, encouraging a voyeuristic, potentially sadistic attitude towards the female body.

Thus Sheila Redmond expresses a visceral reaction to Lutkenhause-Lackey's *Crucified Woman*. 'It sent shivers down my spine,' she writes – but not in a positive way. 'It is not enough that women are battered, bruised, raped, and otherwise denied a reality, it must now be glorified as suffering for the greater good.'[48] Other women, particularly those who have experienced physical or sexual abuse, have found the image profoundly healing and liberating. An anonymous woman responding to *Crucified Woman* wrote:

> O God,
> through the image of a woman
> crucified on the cross
> I understand at last.
>
> For over half of my life
> I have been ashamed
> of the scars I bear . . .

The writer goes on to explain how the image of Christ as a woman has enabled her to know God's presence at the heart of her violation and suffering. She concludes:

> You were not ashamed of your wounds . . .
> I will no longer hide these wounds of mine.
> I will bear them gracefully.
> They tell a resurrection story.[49]

Edwina Hunter, responding to the Edwina Sandys *Christa*, spoke of the sculpture as a 'visual sermon, and, strangely, a sermon of hope':

> No crucifix of Jesus I have ever seen has preached to me with the power of the *original reality* as does the Christa. No sermon in words I have ever heard preached has moved me to such oneness with all my crucified sisters everywhere – whatever their color, race, nationality, or economic standing.[50]

The mixed reactions to the figure of the crucified Christa raise important theological as well as cultural and psychological questions, some of which are powerfully put by Ivone Gebara in her reflections on the Edwina Sandys sculpture:

> Why should the naked body of a crucified man be an object of veneration while that of a woman be judged pornographic? Why should

the body of a crucified man become a symbol of reconciliation and that of a woman treated as a cause of separation and argument within the community? Will women by reason of their sex be excluded from any capacity for salvation? What value does the cross have for women?[51]

The image of the crucified Christa, we might say, focuses for us in a particularly sharp way a number of questions with which feminist Christology has to wrestle. First, and obviously, there is the gender question: how far is Christology limited and constrained by the biological masculinity of the historical Jesus, or, as Ruether famously put it, 'Can a male saviour save women?'[52] By no means all feminist theologians are convinced that a female Christ is either necessary or helpful for women. Some see the masculinity of Jesus as important because Jesus represents a form of masculinity that precisely challenges and undermines patriarchal notions of power and, in his death, exposes and undercuts the male symbolic.[53] Second, there is a question about the centrality of the cross in Christology, and how far the suffering and death of a saviour figure (whether male or female) is essential to the meaning and efficacy of Christianity. Feminists have been at the forefront of a thoroughgoing critique of traditional atonement theology which has seen the death of Christ as necessary for the salvation of humanity, suggesting that Christianity, in its idolization of the cross, has been a death-fixated and violence-mongering religion. A female Christ dying a violent death on the cross may be no more salvific than a male saviour (I return to these questions below). Third, there is a question concerning how far Christianity needs an individual saviour figure at the centre of its symbol system, or whether, as some of the feminist theologians quoted above suggest, we need to move away from thinking in terms of an isolated heroic type of Christ to think much more of a corporate, communal Christ who is known in the body of believers, not fixed in the image or story of one particular man at a certain point in history.

These are all profound questions which require sustained theological attention, and I cannot hope to address them adequately in a book of this nature – yet they are some of the questions, alongside others, that have occupied me as I have explored the theme of the Christa, and it is questions such as these that underlie many of the poems and pieces that make up the body of the book.

Biblical and historical roots of the Christa

The idea of a female Christ is not as new as many might think. Although the notion of the Christa has only taken specific shape in recent decades in the context of second-wave feminism, earlier forms of the female Christ figure can be traced in the history of Christian tradition – in popular forms of piety, in orthodox theology as well as in so-called 'heretical' movements outside the mainstream of doctrinal patriarchy. Moreover, these traditions themselves did not appear out of nowhere, and can be seen as legitimate expressions of earlier scriptural Christology, even if the notion of a female Christ is not one that we find explicitly in Scripture itself. Or perhaps we should not even say that, for Jesus certainly called on feminine imagery to speak about himself, his work, the person and work of the Spirit, and God – and these are some of the roots of the later image of the Christa. Here, then, I will point to some of the biblical roots of the idea of the Christa, before going on to highlight some examples of a female Christ from the history of Christian tradition.

Starting with Jesus himself, although there is some dispute concerning the precise nature of Jesus' attitudes towards women, his incorporation of women into his teaching and practice, and so on, it cannot be disputed that Jesus is presented in the Gospels using feminine imagery about himself – for example, likening himself to a mother hen gathering her chicks (Luke 13.34), as well as using feminine imagery to speak of the work of God or of the Spirit (e.g., Luke 13.20–21; 15.8–10; John 3.3). Whereas, as I have previously shown,[54] his parables are very largely drawn from a patriarchal world of male actors and concerns, nevertheless, the parables that we do have drawn from women's experience are highly significant insofar as they show a creative theological mind that deliberately employs female categories to speak of God and the reign of God.

John's Gospel, in particular, is densely layered with feminine imagery, especially maternal imagery, although this has generally been passed over or not noticed in Johannine studies until feminist biblical scholars alerted attention to it.[55] Birthing and mothering imagery pervade the whole Gospel, from the Prologue through to the Passion and Resurrection narratives, with details that are unique to John opening up a distinct theology of the death of Jesus as the gateway to new

18

life. In the Prologue to the Gospel, the birthing of the creation, the *Logos* and the children of God are interconnected and, at 1.13, the mention of blood links to the crucifixion scene of 19.34 where blood and water flow from Jesus' open side – surely an image of birth from the womb of Jesus, especially when read in the light of other references in the Gospel to new birth from above (3.1–21), the living waters that gush forth from the womb (4.4–42, 7.37–39) and Jesus' labour pangs in birthing a renewed people of God (16.21). The presence of Jesus' mother as midwife to his public ministry (2.1–11) and at the cross to witness his death as the opening of the birth canal toward eternal life confirms the centrality of maternal imagery throughout the Gospel. Finally, in the resurrection appearances, uniquely in John, Jesus breathes on the disciples. Barbara Reid comments, 'Just as the midwife attending the birth of a child may blow breath into its nostrils to help it breathe on its own, so Jesus breathes the breath of the Spirit on his disciples, enabling them to go out on their own, extending his life-giving mission.'[56]

In all four gospel traditions, the resurrection stories, enigmatic as they are and difficult to synthesize, lay the foundations for a Christology which takes with ultimate seriousness the strangeness of the risen Christ. There is a strong theme throughout the resurrection appearances of Christ incognito – the risen Christ who is not recognized by the disciples, the one who returns like a 'thief in the night', coming by surprise – suggesting that the forms the Christ will take are novel, strange, unrecognized, subversive, pushing the boundaries of the known and familiar. If we think we know who the Christ is, what he looks like and when and how he will appear, we are of all people most deluded.

There is, of course, the whole biblical tradition of Wisdom, represented in late biblical Jewish thought as a female figure, from the feminine form of the Hebrew *Hokma*, which was applied to Christ in early Christian thought as one highly creative means of understanding how Christ was active in creation and history. Thus, for example, the Johannine Prologue (John 1.1–18) is modelled very closely on biblical texts about Wisdom, but the term *Sophia* is not actually used, replaced instead by the Word, or *Logos* – a masculine term that was much in use in Greek philosophy, so that, very early in Christian tradition, the radical gender significance of Christ as female Wisdom became lost and repressed. It is only in our own time

19

that the figure of Wisdom is receiving a great deal of attention from biblical scholars and others, not least because of the scholarship of feminists which has retrieved this largely neglected tradition to the centre of Jewish and Christian consciousness.[57] The Christa, we might say, is one manifestation of a retrieved Wisdom Christology.

The Pauline notion of the Church as the 'body of Christ' is another New Testament theme which suggests that the risen Christ is no longer to be identified with the historical Jesus but is to be encountered in the company of those who are baptized in his name. Paul, indeed, seems quite proud of the fact that he did not know the historical Jesus, and his claim to apostleship relies entirely on his encounter with the risen Christ. In speaking of the body of Christ, Paul is of course referring to the community and not to individuals as such, as Romans 12 makes very clear; nevertheless, such language certainly suggests a strong identification between the believer and Christ such that it is not inconceivable to think of the individual believer as one who may, in a real sense, represent Christ. Indeed, Paul implies this when he calls on the Christians at Corinth to 'be imitators of me, as I am of Christ' (1 Corinthians 11.1). This notion of the individual believer being the representative of Christ is found again and again in Christian tradition, perhaps most aptly summarized in Teresa of Avila's famous saying, 'Christ has no body now on earth but yours, no hands, no feet on earth but yours. Yours are the eyes through which is to look out Christ's compassion to the world.'[58] If 'Christ has no body now on earth but yours', then it follows that Christ can now be found and imaged in a multiplicity of forms – black and white, male and female, gay and straight, to note but a few of the manifestations in which we do, in fact, find Christ imaged.

Moving beyond the biblical era, we find multiple evidence of Christ being experienced, and spoken about, in feminine imagery from the earliest times. Thus in medieval mysticism, as well as in the Patristics, Jesus was quite frequently imaged in maternal imagery, and this in a highly concrete, embodied way. Julian of Norwich, among many others, images Jesus as the Mother who gives birth to the believer through his own body, and also as the lactating Mother who feeds believers with his own body in the sacrament, as a mother feeds her child with her breast.[59] The wound in the side of Christ was frequently imaged as a breast by the medievals, and also as a semi-open vulva. Visual portrayals of the wounds of Christ make this quite clear.[60] At the same time, there is a dynamic interdependent relationship between Christ thus imaged as female and the female saint or mystic whose body is closely associated with that of Christ. Thus, many medieval holy women were reputed to lactate like Christ, and offered their breast milk to the faithful as an embodied sacrament. There are tales of people going on pilgrimage to suck at the breasts of holy women. Not only, then, is Christ imaged as female in these spiritual traditions, but the female body is identified as Christlike, as Christic.[61] Even where feminine imagery was not used, the debate about gender in Christology was a live one; many medieval theologians discussed whether Christ might have been born a woman and, though they all conclude in favour of his masculinity, it is instructive that they do not find the question nonsensical and come up with a range of reasons why Christ was born a male.[62]

Ruether points to a variety of groups in Christian tradition that developed the ideal of an androgynous Christ, or a Christ manifested in both male *and* female form. The Shakers, for example, proposed a female Messiah who stands alongside, and is equivalent in status and significance to, Christ. For the Shakers, the female Christ is the theological expression of the androgyny of God and God's image, humanity, which must be expressed in a redeemer from both the male and the female orders of humanity. The female as the last of God's works is the crowning glory of creation. So the appearance of the female Christ in Mother Ann Lee, the founder of the Shaker sect, is necessary to complete and perfect the redemptive revelation of God who is both Father and Mother.[63]

As well as such theological roots to the *idea* of a female Christ figure, we also find an iconographic precedent for the Christa in the ancient tradition of the female, crucified martyr – particularly as represented in the Wilgefortis tradition, but also exemplified in stories and images of other female martyrs such as St Julia and St Eulalia. Here we find in Christian art and devotion the repeated image of a suffering, crucified female form, who is not Christ as such – although, taking seriously the capacity of the saint to image or represent Christ, we might see such figures as *in persona christae*, those who represent in their own broken bodies and poured out blood the suffering of Christ. We might also see these female saints as another example of the repressed feminine divine coming to some kind of consciousness in Christianity, alongside devotion to Mary. Whatever their theological significance, these figures of a crucified female form certainly provide an iconographic tradition within which we may place more recent manifestations of the crucified woman.

Although hardly known to contemporary Christians, Wilgefortis is foremost among this company of female crucified martyrs. The legend of Wilgefortis (otherwise known as Uncumber, Ontcommer, Kümmernis or Liberata) tells of how the pious noblewoman converted to Christianity and wished to dedicate her life to prayer and contemplation. Her father, having other ideas, had promised her in marriage to a pagan king. Wilgefortis prayed that God would make her so repulsive to her suitor that he would break the engagement, thus enabling her to keep her vow of celibacy. The Lord answered her prayer, she sprouted a beard, and the engagement was called off. Her father, outraged, crucified her. The cult of Wilgefortis was extremely popular in the fourteenth century, extending across Europe to England, France, Italy, Spain and Holland, and being particularly strong in Germany and Austria. She was venerated by those seeking relief from their troubles, and particularly by women who wished to be liberated (unencumbered) from abusive husbands. Although many of her images were destroyed at the Reformation, and her cult largely forgotten (officially suppressed in 1969), images of the bearded crucified saint can still be found scattered across Europe, including a carving in the Henry VII chapel of Westminster Abbey.[64]

The idea of the female Christ, then, while shocking and even offensive to some contemporary Christians, has a noble and ancient pedigree and is a tradition with serious spiritual and theological intent (although, as I have noted, it can also be employed in more playful, parodic and, yes, sometimes offensive, ways – though the nature of the offence is not in the association of the female body with Christ, but in the sexualized, objectified and abusive ways in which the female Christic body is portrayed or described). Of course, the idea of a female Christ need not, in and of itself, be a liberating one. Feminist theologians have critiqued the female Christ for being essentialist, for reinforcing stereotypical and limiting notions of the feminine, especially the idea of the feminine as nurturing, motherly and sacrificial love, and for objectifying the female body as an object of male desire, power and voyeurism. A female Christ needs to be as open to critique, nuance, dialogue and difference as any of the previous male Christs have been – or should have been. As Heyward, Nakashima Brock and others have suggested, an exclusive focus on an individual heroic figure, whether male or female, is not empowering in the long run. The symbol of the Christa will only be liberating and life-giving if it is held tensively, critically and with awareness of the idolizing tendencies human beings are apt to bring to any and every image of the divine.

My own exploration of the Christa

Although I have been aware of the Christa for many years,[65] I have become deeply fascinated by this figure over the past few years, as one contemporary manifestation of the search for the feminine divine, particularly since helping to facilitate a women's alternative Holy Week and Easter retreat in 2006. It was this event that sparked off my exploration for forms of the *risen* Christa. At that gathering, a group of some dozen or so women came together in our own self-catering cottage in the grounds of the RSHM Retreat Centre at Noddfa, Penmaenmawr, North Wales. We gathered on Maundy Thursday for the Triduum, making our own liturgy to mark the journey through the three traditionally most holy days in the Christian calendar, remembering Jesus' last days and the birth of the early Church in the Easter experience. In a variety of ways we explored the different associations, meanings, questions, challenges and insights we brought to our diverse theological traditions of Passiontide and Easter. We endeavoured to live together in a collaborative, mutually enriching way, sharing the work, the planning and organizing of liturgy, as well as social times together, with minimal and dispersed leadership, respecting each other's differences as well as the bonds of friendship and solidarity that bound us.

It was a powerful and renewing time for each one of us, and, although I didn't realize it at the time, those few days served as the catalyst for an ongoing process of exploration and creativity that has culminated in this book. As part of our Holy Week liturgy, we worked with the image of the Christa – a familiar image to some of us and brand new (startlingly, shockingly new, even) to others. We painted the Christa, we wrote poems and prayers about her, we discussed our understanding of her theological and spiritual significance, we argued about her. It was in the context of this shared reflection and prayer that, together, we posed the question: 'Where is the risen Christa?' 'Why are all the forms of the Christa that have been so significant to feminist theology suffering, crucified figures?' For it is the case that, to date, almost all of the theological interest in the Christa figure, and almost all of the artistic representations, have centred on a *crucified* woman. (A couple of notable exceptions are the joyous image of a female Christ figure at Emmaus by the Filipina artist Emmanuel Garibay which forms the cover image of this book[66] and Jill Ansell's reworking of Matthias Grünewald's image of the risen Christ on the Isenheim altarpiece as a female figure[67] – but none of us had discovered these images at that 2006 retreat. Also, depictions of Christ as the female figure of Wisdom, such as those by Robert Lentz and William Hart McNichols,[68] offer an alternative vision of the Christa which is not focused on suffering.)

Perhaps the dominance of the suffering and crucified female form reflects the need many feminist women feel to identify with a symbol that speaks to and of their pain, oppression and negation by patriarchal religion; but as we gathered together at Noddfa in 2006, a number of us who were part of that gathering expressed the need for an image and understanding of a *risen* Christa. This quest for a risen Christa has motivated the present exploration. I am in search of symbols of the feminine divine which can speak to and of women's risenness, strength, power, vitality and liveliness, our quest for life in all its fullness – without ignoring or obliterating the wounds and without denying the realities of evil, sin and death. This search connects with directions taken by a number of feminists who, in a variety of ways, challenge what Mary Daly has termed the 'necrophiliac' fixation of Christianity,[69] who question the dominance of the cross within traditional understandings of salvation and atonement and particular ways of conceptualizing the death of Jesus that lay stress on his vicarious and innocent suffering, and who seek for more biophiliac ways of thinking about redemption, employing categories of natality and flourishing to suggest alternative models of salvation.[70]

Thus it is important to ask how helpful is the image of a crucified woman to replace that of a crucified man on the cross? While this may have its place within a repertoire of images of the Christa, by itself it is not enough and it may well be as limiting as previous traditional images of the cross. As Ivone Gebara puts it, 'While not denying the truth of the cross of Jesus and of all crosses, feminist theology contributes to the opening of life and thought to a sense of solidarity, in the cross and beyond it.[71] Gebara argues that it is necessary to speak of many crosses, including the crosses of women, when we speak of the cross of Jesus:

> One cross cannot contain all sufferings or all crosses. It would risk founding an empire of suffering, even if the end were to found the empire of love. Absolutizing the cross of Jesus is completely under-standable in the context of the political theocentrism of the Middle Ages, but it has become problematic in our actual history. Even if we speak of God crucified, we deal with absolutizing one particular type of suffering and one type of manifestation of the divinity. Hence the importance of holding the memory of the crucified Jesus together with the memory of others crucified, men and women alike.[72]

At the same time as widening our concept of the cross, Gebara wants to focus more attention on the resurrection – understood in a decidedly this-worldly and bodily way, located in the here and now (even if the here and now does not exhaust the full meaning of salvation) – what she calls 'Everyday resurrections'.[73]

> In Christian language this is to say that a process of salvation is a process of resurrection, of recovering life and hope and justice along life's path even when these experiences are frail and fleeting. Resurrection becomes something that can be lived and grasped within the confines of our existence.[74]

Thus Gebara speaks powerfully of the search for salvation which has to be renewed each day, in the same way as 'every day we have to begin again the actions of eating and drinking'.[75] Salvation is not a once-and-for-all absolute, but

> a movement toward redemption in the midst of the trials of existence, one moment of peace and tenderness in the midst of daily violence, beautiful music that calms our spirit, a novel that keeps us company, a glass of beer or a cup of coffee shared with another.[76]

'Salvation is a get-together, an event, a sentiment, a kiss, a piece of bread, a happy old woman.'[77] If these seem rather mundane, ephemeral and partial glimpses of salvation, perhaps they are, and perhaps that is the only way we can touch risenness in our own day-to-day lives.

Marcella Althaus-Reid also writes suggestively about the resurrection of Christ in terms of Mary Daly's notion of 'wonderlust', an intense longing, craving, eagerness and enthusiasm for life. Resurrection is a lusty, embodied, political experience rooted in real personal and sexual relationships, as well as in the struggle for justice:

> Christ's resurrected presence can only be seen then as a craving, an enthusiastic passion for life and justice, in the diversity and unfenced identity which is searching for that land called *Basileia* by European theologians and 'the project of liberation of the kingdom' by Latin Americans, in which we are all called to be co-workers. We join then Christ's resurrection with our own coming out for the obscene Christ in a per/verted Christology which reminds us of the ethical need for resurrection.[78]

With Gebara, Althaus-Reid and other feminist and womanist theologians, I want to search for salvation in the everyday and in experiences of here-and-now resurrection, without limiting their meanings to the this-worldly. Even if salvation does extend beyond this life, this is the only life we have to live and this life and this world must be the focus of our discipleship. We can leave whatever other life and worlds there are to come to the one who is to come. I want to look for the risen Christa walking among the ordinary women and men in the world as we know it, in all its beauty, fragility, imperfection and glory. In particular, I am in search of symbols and narratives that will help me, and other women, claim and live into our power – something that I, and many women, seem to struggle with. In saying this, I am of course not uncritical of existing notions of power and affirm with many feminists the need to rethink power in ways that are collaborative, inclusive, non-competitive and anti-hierarchical. Perhaps one of the reasons that women in the Church have struggled and continue to struggle to claim and own our own power and use it in mutually empowering ways is that we do not have many symbols or narratives of authentic female power in our tradition. The risen Christa may be one such reworked symbol that can speak to our need and help call out our own collective power.

At the same time as looking for forms of a risen Christa, I want to push the boundaries of the notion of the Christa in other directions, too, in company with radical feminist and queer theologians. For even as feminist theologians and artists have 'queered' and subverted the patriarchal assumption of the male Christ by offering the alternative image of the female Christ, they have frequently, perhaps unwittingly, adopted and mirrored other assumptions about the identity of the Christ. The Christa may challenge our notions about the gender of God, but all too often images of the Christa have reinforced cultural stereotypes of beauty and bodily perfection. Just as Christ has so often been imaged as an ideal type who encapsulates what a particular culture and society envisages to be the 'perfect body' – male, young, white, lean, powerful and so on – so the Christa may also, unwittingly, reinforce conventions of ideal feminine beauty which may not be all that liberating for women and girls. The Christa to date has been a slender, almost always white and young figure, conforming to cultural notions of the body beautiful.[79] While broken on the cross, nevertheless she seems to mirror the image of the slim, 'perfect', young and nubile body of the white supermodels that stride the fashion catwalks. Where is the fat Christa, Christa in a wheelchair, the blind Christa, the black or Asian Christa? It is all too easy for white, middle-class and able-bodied feminists to reinforce our own limited notions of race, class and body image on Christ, even as we think we are breaking the mould in other ways.

In this book, then, I am working with the idea of the Christa in a number of different ways, gratefully acknowledging the work that feminists and artists before me have done in imaging a female Christ figure, reaching back into more ancient history and traditions to resource my own explorations, but also trying to do something new. This book is, as far as I know, the first book to be wholly dedicated to the figure of the Christa, although other books and articles, as surveyed above, have explored the significance of the idea. It is certainly the first book to explore the notion of the Christa through the medium of poetry, as well as prose – a medium that I find myself using increasingly, as a way of writing a kind of 'vernacular theology' that employs discourse that is both imaginative and conceptual, concrete and narrative, popular and capable of engaging with theory. It is, also, I think, the first work that has applied the idea of the Christa in a detailed way to the whole Passiontide story, offering a series of liturgical and personal prayer resources for Passiontide and Easter. Furthermore, in seeking to image a risen Christa, it is the first serious theological exploration of the Christa that attempts to push beyond the primary manifestation of the Christa as a suffering, crucified figure.

The shape of the book

The shape of the book largely follows the traditional shape of Passiontide and Eastertide, and this is no accident, since the book grew out of just such a liturgical celebration of the Triduum. Thus the heart of the book charts the sequence of events that begin with Maundy Thursday (the foot-washing, the Last Supper, the agony and watch in the garden, the arrest), moves through Good Friday (trial, scourging, cross and death) and Holy Saturday (deposition, laying in the tomb, the waiting in the place of death) and emerges in Easter Sunday (empty tomb, resurrection appearances, transformation of the disciples). In these central chapters, the Passion narrative is re-engaged from the perspective of a female Christ figure, as well as drawing on contemporary women's experiences – including my own – to reflect on the meaning of the gospel events for women and men today.

Around the central Passiontide and Easter focus of the book, I have added brief chapters that allude to other parts of the Christian narrative and the liturgical year. Thus, the first chapter after this one considers nativity and incarnation before we move into the moment of Maundy Thursday, and, following the longest chapter focusing on the quest for a risen Christa, the final chapter looks to the on-going trajectory of the Christian narrative to Ascension, Pentecost and the kin-dom of Christa. A series of collects addressed to Christa are gathered at the end of the book.

Throughout the book, poems, prayers and meditations on the figure of the Christa interweave with more obviously personal reflections on my own life and remembered incidents from the original Noddfa retreat. Sometimes, I start with the religious symbol and story and work with that, trying to enter it and walk around in it, meditating on it and finding ways in which it may speak to me – not always confirming my own experience and expectations, I hope; sometimes challenging and confronting my prejudices and aspirations. Like any reflection on Scripture that is to be worth anything, I don't go there merely to have my own theology confirmed – although of course there is always the danger of reading my own meanings into Scripture and religious symbols, and some may feel that is exactly what I have done with my reflections on the Christa. I hope there is more than that here, but that is something others will have to judge.

And sometimes, I start more obviously with my own experience, with my life as it is, in all its mundane ups and downs, occasionally touched by larger crises, sufferings and ecstasies – bringing these into dialogue with the Christian narrative and seeing what the interaction between life and Christian tradition, albeit newly expressed in regendered ways, might evoke.

From whichever end the dialogue starts – from the 'objective' side of Scripture, tradition, liturgy and religious symbol, or from the 'subjective' side of my life, experience, feelings, questions and searchings – the hope is for a genuinely creative and dynamic bringing together of life and faith, in order for new insight and wisdom, practical spiritual wisdom, to be born, so that both faith and life may be refreshed. The ways in which Christians and theologians speak of Christ, symbolize Christ, visualize Christ, and pray to Christ in liturgy and prayer – all of these seem to me absolutely crucial to our own quest for personal and social redemption, wholeness and fullness of life. Christologies can speak to us of a God incarnate in our own fleshy, messy lives and struggling with us in our work, loves, joys and hopes towards more expansive and joyous life – or they can mirror discourses that restrict, limit and literally crucify women's bodies, becoming part of the symbolic order against which women need to fight and protest. I am aiming towards a feminist Christology that is emancipatory, joyous, subversive, playful yet deeply serious too: a Christology that is real about suffering, death and pain yet resists absorption into these realities or passive acceptance of them; a Christology knitted from the fragments of my life and the lives of the others with whom I am intimately, and sometimes less closely, connected; worked from meditation and reflection on the Scriptures, particularly the Gospels, and also from wider Christian tradition, particularly the history of women's spirituality, prayer and theologies; and drawing from contemporary culture, whether Christian or not, particularly in the form of visual works of art representing the Christa, but also from wider poetry and fiction which might offer glimpses of a risen Christa.

What I am *not* trying to do in any of this is rewrite history, in the sense of imagining or pretending that the Jesus of history might have been a woman and what the course of Christianity might have looked like had this been so. This is clearly an anachronistic fantasy, and I have no interest in denying the historical particularity of the man

Jesus or the first-century Palestinian world he inhabited. Rather, I am working at the level of symbol, as poets and storytellers do, and seeking to dialogue with the tradition in order to re-engage it in fresh ways, rather as an artist may seek to paint Jesus in a time and a society far removed from first-century Nazareth – not in order to reduce or belittle the original setting and man but in order to discover ways in which that original story can speak freshly in new settings and times. In such a rewriting or re-painting of the tradition, it is the juxtaposition of the ancient tradition with the new setting and perspective that has the potential to create fresh perspectives and insight.

Although poets do not usually follow academics in supplying copious footnotes to their poems, I have included substantial notes at the end of the book, not only to the prose discussions but also to the poems themselves (but note that, after this chapter, notes are unnumbered so as not to intrude upon the reading of the poems). There is a danger in this, of course: that the notes will somehow 'tell' the reader how to interpret the poems, rather than letting them speak for themselves and letting the reader do their own work of meaning-making. I do not intend the notes in this fashion, but rather to point to some of the sources and motivating ideas that lie behind the poems so that readers can, should they wish, follow these up for themselves.

In this collection, then, I want to go in search of a risen Christa in company with others who have sought her presence, yet pushing beyond the boundaries already delineated by feminist theologians and artists into fresh spaces and possibilities. In doing so, I hope to bring new insights and perspectives to bear on the (to some) very familiar gospel stories about Jesus and the liturgical practices that mark out the Easter season and, at the same time, by bringing Christology into dialogue with feminism, to illuminate the realities of women's lives in new and creative ways.

2

Come as a girl

Nativity and incarnation

There's a feminist cartoon which did the rounds as a Christmas card, perhaps a couple of decades ago now, showing Mary and Joseph in the stable, with the crib centre stage. Mary has a startled look on her face as she gazes into the crib, and the speech bubble declares, 'It's a girl!' The cartoon worked precisely because it *was* shocking – and still is to many – to imagine Christ coming as a girl; but our own surprise and laughter at the very idea is instructive, and having laughed at the cartoon we might find ourselves a few seconds later wondering why. There's another, rather less well-known version of this joke, which tells how God *did* come as a girl, and no one took the slightest bit of notice of anything she said or did, nothing got passed on or written down, so God had to start again and send a boy. And the rest is history. This joke, which appears in a variety of manifestations, is hardly original – it is another variation on Virginia Woolf's fantasy of Shakespeare's sister, Judith. In *A Room of One's Own*, Woolf invented the character of Judith to demonstrate how a woman with the same creative genius as the famous bard would never have been able to get any of her works into print or on the stage, and thus would have been consigned to oblivion, however great her literary merits. So maybe the idea of a Christa born two thousand years ago whom no one has ever heard about is not so unthinkable? Actually, theologians from earliest times debated with all seriousness whether God *could* have 'come as a girl' and certainly in the Middle Ages, this was a lively debate. As Janet Martin Soskice puts it, 'The conclusion, that it was fitting that Christ be born a man, was never in doubt, yet the arguments are worth noting by anyone interested in the symbolics of sex.' After reviewing a variety of these arguments, Soskice comes to the most common one, typified by Aquinas in the *Summa Theologiae*: 'Because the male excels the female sex, Christ assumed a man's nature' – though this is balanced by the additional comment, 'So that people should not think little of the female sex, it was fitting that he should take flesh from a woman.' Even while the great theologian attempts to retain respect for female flesh, it is clear that he still thinks, as does the little girl in her letter to God, that 'boys are best'.

Whatever the jokes and the arguments, the creative act of imagining Christa as a *girl*, and not only a woman, is important for a number of reasons. Feminist theology has, with some justification, been criticized for paying scant attention to the situation, needs and gifts of girls, although this is gradually changing. Perhaps in the early decades of feminism, when women were deconstructing the gendered roles of wife and mother which had been their lot for centuries, it is understandable that their focus should have been on their own lives, independent from consideration of the lives of their children. However, since it is the girl who becomes the woman, it is self-evident that feminism must pay close attention to the situation and needs of girls, and likewise, feminist theology must give serious study to the faith of girls – as it is now beginning to do. Although, at our Easter gathering at Noddfa, we were a bunch of adult women, and didn't really think about Christa as a girl, subsequently, in the development of this book, it has become important for me to extend the narrative backwards, so to speak, and consider the birth and origins and growing pains of the Christa, as a way of considering the gifts and needs of girls and young women in our churches and world today.

Although the chapter starts here, with the challenge to imagine Christ coming as a girl, it doesn't end there. The final few pieces begin to move into adult territory, and intimate what is to come as they meditate on a Christa in the form of a despised and rejected suffering servant, and a Christa exiled into the wilderness.

Come as a girl

Come as a girl.
I did. Nobody noticed.

Come as a girl.
I do. Open your eyes, your mind, your stoppered ears.

Come as a girl.
I will. I am still arriving among you,
looking for a safe place to be born,
a welcome, a home.

Christa, becoming

*'The girl is to be considered as the becoming of the becoming woman,
and of all becomings.'*   Marcella Althaus-Reid

1

Come as a girl
on your way to becoming
not knowing wholly who you are yet
Come as the becoming of becomings

Come as the girl giving up on childhood
though choosing to return there if she will
leaving behind her toys or finding new ones
fearful perhaps of losing the safe, free space of the girl-child

Come as the girl who knows about
the fear of taking on the weight of womanhood
as one who has walked beside

Alice, sixteen, who cuts herself to find temporary relief
from the internal pain that is too great to bear

Sally, fourteen, who is starving her softly rounding body
afraid of taking up too much space in the world
erasing herself in the world of her elders

Katie, eighteen, who has flunked out of her first year at
    university
she's too clever by half and afraid of her cleverness

Madeleine, nineteen, who works on the streets
to support her habit and her four-year-old daughter
she can't remember how she came to be here

Alyssia, fifteen, who was beautiful and talented and
everybody thought she was happy and going places
until her body was found hanging from the banisters

Come as the girl
refusing the foreclosures of womanhood
the dead ends of domesticity
erasures of ethereal spirituality
mausoleums of mass-produced femininity

Come as the   wild child
                bi-girl
                free child
                boys own
                god child
                live-wire
                fire child
                god girl
                glad boy
                womanish self you care to become

2

Come as Jairus's daughter
waking up from your premature death on the cusp
   of adolescence
no longer afraid to bleed
Show us the womanly well-being of God

Come as Miriam
using your persuasion to convince the princess
to protect the baby brother you could not care for yourself
defying the death-dealing law of the state
Show us God's transgressive deliverance

Come as Lo-ruhamah
the not-to-be-pitied who is pitied
the not-to-be-loved whose mother loves her
Show us the girl with her own name whose
destiny prefigures the salvation of her people

Come as the girl trafficked across borders
to serve as slave to a foreign mistress
whose spirited counsel brings healing to those who
    oppress her
Show us the wisdom of the little ones
which humbles the mighty and mends the afflicted

3

Come as the girl
learning to act grown-up, responsible, in charge

Come as the girl
who loves music, dance, the moon,
the Spirit, food, roundness, struggle, the folk

Come as the girl
not forgetting how to be outrageous
audacious, courageous and wilful

Come as the girl who loves herself
                          regardless

Christa growing up
Ezekiel 16.1–7

Though your origin and birth were in a foreign land,
your father and mother strangers to each other,
yet I have chosen you.

Though on the day of your birth your navel cord was not cut,
nor were you washed with water to cleanse you,
nor wrapped in clothes to protect you,
yet I will deliver you and bear you up.

Though you were abhorred on the day you were born
and thrown out to die in the open field,
flailing about in your blood,
yet I will lift you out of your misery
and have compassion on the abandoned one.

Though your life was regarded as worthless,
your girl-child's body expendable,
yet I shall say to you:
Live! And grow up like a plant of the field.

Though none expected you to survive,
and none looked to you to flourish,
yet I shall watch you grow tall, your breasts forming,
until you arrive at full womanhood.

And there you shall live as you choose.

The sisters of famous men

Jesus had a sister, Esther, as passionate and clever as he was.
She could not go to synagogue or learn from the rabbis.
So, gleaning what she could from her brother,
they'd stay up late at night, whispering about the latest interpretation
of the Scriptures and whether a good Jew
was compelled always to obey the Romans.
He had his heart set on preaching.
She longed to go with him, but Joseph had other plans,
and had already betrothed her to an apprentice from his workshop.
Late one night, she slipped out of the compound,
carrying her few belongings,
and made her way to Jerusalem.
Hanging around the Temple, the priests shooed her away
back to the women's quarters.
Drunk pilgrims made passes at her.
Too frightened to think what to do,
she felt only relief when some girls from a Nazareth family
recognized her and offered to take her back with them next day.
Home again, only twenty-four hours later, she had to endure a beating,
her mother's tears and the teasing of her siblings.
Joseph brought the date of her marriage forward.
In twelve months she was settled in a village down the road
and delivered of her firstborn. She didn't see much of Jesus.

A litany for the young who dare to grow up different

Young lad growing up in a mining town in County Durham,
whose only passion is to dance;
your da' and your brother want to knock the hell
out of Thatcher's government
and out of your strange ambitions.
Go Billy, go!
Live! And grow up like a plant of the field.

Anne of Green Gables,
with your carrot-coloured locks and your endless scrapes,
you tried the patience of Marilla
but never gave up on your dream to be a writer.
Live! And grow up like a plant of the field.

Jamal Malik, you made it off the rubbish heaps of Mumbai,
swimming through shit,
jumping off trains,
daring death in the alleyways of the street-vendors,
pimps and money grabbers,
to make your million.
Live! And grow up like a plant of the field.

Paikea Apirana, last of the descendants of the Whale Rider,
you recovered the whale tooth from the sea
and rode the great whale on the waters,
claiming your right to be the first female leader of your
    people.
Live! And grow up like a plant of the field.

All you young heroes, heroines, misfits, unlikely saviours,
holding on to your vision and talents and dreams:
refusing to give up, as others have,
surviving parents' mockery, siblings' disbelief, elders' reproof:
Live! And grow up like a plant of the field.

No oil painting
Isaiah 53.2b

We're not fussy, could go for blonde, brunette, raven,
and not only the conventional type: our tastes are broad.
But her! She wasn't the kind of woman you'd fantasize
    about –
or only in your bad dreams. Lumpy legs,
hairs on her lip she didn't even attempt to wax,
an angry rash down one side of her face and neck.
Big, clumsy hands that were always dropping things
and an awkward, uncoordinated gait.
If you looked at her twice in the street it was not beauty that
    compelled you
but a look as if she were haunted, or hunted.
Even so, her gaze didn't turn away when you gawped at her,
as any decent woman's would have done:
she stared you out, daring your revulsion,
till you moved on, shaking the memory of the strange
    encounter off,
home to your wife or girlfriend, or some warm bar
where there would be plenty of lookers to help you forget.
No, not a face you'd want hanging on your walls
or, God forbid, adorning your churches.

Christa in the wilderness

She had left some time ago.
Driven out into places of exposure
by a hunger for the solace of fierce landscapes,
she set off for abandoned wastelands on the edge of urban
    development,
loitered in railway sidings and along canal towpaths,
paced city rubbish tips and derelict factory sites,
walked for miles around council estates
in government-forsaken former mill towns.

No one would think to look for her here, she thought.
Few, if any, recognized her.
Mostly, folk left her alone, sensing her taste for solitude.
Occasionally children approached, to talk
or offer stolen goods or ask for money.
Dogs, with or without owners, snapped at her heels,
looking as if they might bite.
Once, at dusk, some men high on dope bore down on her.
She carried on walking, looking ahead. They parted
like perfectly choreographed dancers, letting her go.

She walked her way along six-lane highways where the traffic
juddered and honked and slapped against her body.
She breathed in the stench of exhaust fumes,
crunched broken glass underfoot on the hard shoulder.

She had no sense of where she was going.
She wasn't going anywhere.
She needed to look on expanses that would hurt her eyes,
wouldn't offer comfort.
She needed a quality of rawness, smells that seeped into
    her body
and drove her on, gasping for clean air.
She didn't want trees or foliage with their promise of oasis.
She wanted absence, endlessly extending horizons,
a featureless, colourless topography
like an empty abstract canvas across which she could travel
    unhidden.

3

The table of women

Maundy Thursday

Passiontide begins on Palm Sunday, when traditionally the entire Passion narrative is read dramatically in churches as a kind of overview of and preparation for all that is to follow. The start of Holy Week signals a deeper entry into the events of Jesus' last days; in solemn Eucharists, often accompanied by addresses, the events leading up to Jesus' betrayal and arrest are recalled. As the week unfolds, the eve of Maundy Thursday marks yet another liminal moment when the Church enters into the most sombre and intense period of the liturgical year: the Triduum, the period of three days from Holy Thursday to Easter Sunday. These days are the climax, not only of the preceding forty days of Lent, but of the entire Christian calendar, the crux to which everything points and from which everything proceeds.

Although different denominations and individual churches vary enormously in the manner and style in which they keep each element of the Triduum (if they keep it at all), there are certain common features that have been established from earliest times. So, the Maundy Thursday liturgy comprises the following key features: a eucharistic celebration recalling the Last Supper and the inauguration of the Holy Communion, incorporating the foot-washing, and ending with a procession of the Holy Sacrament to a 'chapel of rest', usually lavishly decorated with flowers; the stripping of the altar, often accompanied by the solemn reading of Psalm 22, and the removal of all lights, icons, statuary and any form of decoration, from the church, leaving the space as bare as possible; the service of watch, in the chapel of rest, during which Jesus' agony in the garden is recalled, and worshippers seek to remain with Christ in his agony.

Feminist liturgists have sought to critique, reinterpret and reclaim each of these features of the liturgy in different ways. Traditional depictions of the Last Supper have, of course, represented Jesus at table with the twelve men: women and children have been notable by their absence – and this has been one of the chief platforms for excluding women from presiding or even serving at the eucharistic table. Feminist historians and liturgists alike have challenged this androcentric reading of the tradition, insisting that women and children habitually shared in the table fellowship of Jesus and that the weight of probability therefore supports their presence at his final meal. As Dorothy A. Lee summarizes the evidence from the Gospels: 'A close reading indicates that a larger group of disciples than the twelve celebrated the Last Supper with Jesus. This group would un-doubtedly have included the women accepted by Jesus into table fellowship.' A number of more recent paintings of the Last Supper include women and children around the table.

Going beyond mere inclusion, feminists have pointed out that the very notion of Eucharist – a feeding of the faithful with the body and blood of the Lord – is rooted in women's experience of childbearing and weaning. It is women, primarily, who know what it is to feed the child birthed from their body with their own very being and substance. Feminist liturgies have therefore sought to reclaim Eucharist as something that women celebrate as part and parcel of their ordinary lives, whether ordained to a ritual priesthood or not. Similarly, women don't need to be taught about the washing and care of bodies; this is something they have done down the cen-turies, and continue to do, both as everyday, domestic service and as the lavish, erotic cherishing of the body of the beloved in intimate lovemaking. Keeping watch at the place of agony and betrayal is another experience that women have known for centuries: as carers of the ill and the dying, as those who know what it is to watch and wait, as those who have remained faithful in prayer.

While feminist theologians and liturgists have sought to reappro-priate the sacraments and feasts of the Church for *all* women and not simply to focus on women clergy or those in leadership, there is an undoubted symbolic significance in the woman priest/presider as one who embodies in a particularly focused ritual way the person and image of a feminine divine. We might see the woman priest/ presbyter, particularly in her role as presiding at the Eucharist, as a mother saviour feeding her children from her own body, a Christa feeding those gathered from her own table. This idea of the woman priest as herself an image of the Christa is one that is suggested and explored by a number of recent studies. Thus, Anita Monro speaks of the density of symbolism that is focused in the act of a woman presiding at the Eucharist: 'The feminine body (Church) is fed with the feminine body (Eucharist) by the feminine body (presider). The female presider is provider for the family. Christ feeds her people with her very self at her own hand.'

At our Noddfa Easter retreat, we gathered on Maundy Thursday as a group of lay women beginning a spiritual journey together and embarking on a shared time of prayer, ritual, meals, relaxation, silence and conversation. Some of us knew others well, as friends, partners and companions; some of us knew perhaps only one other person present. Some of us were well familiar with the traditional celebration of the Triduum, and had also been involved in different forms of liturgical experiment at Easter. Others came from traditions where the Triduum holds a lesser significance, at least in terms of its being marked out as a special liturgical season; others again no longer had contact with mainstream churches. Those of us responsible for planning our first evening together wanted to make it a time of relaxed arrival and settling in, recognizing that people would be tired after long journeys and might feel apprehensive about the coming days; and at the same time, we wanted to mark the moment as one fraught with significance, conscious of Christians throughout the world gathering in different places and ways to remember Jesus' last meal with his friends, to keep watch at his betrayal and arrest. As a group of lay women, there was no one woman to take the role of president or priest; rather, we shared out the leadership and 'holding' of the liturgy in an organic, dispersed way.

So we planned a simple gathering around the kitchen table (a space where women have often gathered to talk, eat and wash up); we made time for introducing ourselves and our hopes for the retreat, we washed each other's hands as a symbol of refreshment and cleansing from our journeys, as well as a remembrance of Jesus' foot-washing. We anointed each other's hands with perfumed oil, recollecting the woman who anointed Jesus for his burial. Then we ate a simple meal together, chatting informally and remembering other Holy Weeks and Easters we had experienced. Afterwards, we processed informally from the house where we were staying into the large, rambling gardens of the retreat centre, making our way to an enclosed garden where we rehearsed the story of Jesus' agony, sang Taizé chants and kept watch in the dark. Some of us walked the labyrinth in the garden as a form of quiet meditation and prayer. There was no formal end to the evening, and people drifted back to the house when they were ready, or stayed outside waiting and praying, as they chose.

In the pieces that follow, I seek to reflect on the many different aspects of the Maundy Thursday liturgy and story – washing, anointing, feeding, watching and waiting – as they are expressed in women's lives in a variety of settings and ways, as well as imagining how a Christa figure, in different times and places, might give expression to these symbolic actions. Some of the pieces recall the time at Noddfa; others refer to other settings in my own life and in the lives of others.

In memory of her

Mark 14.9

We will refuse to stay outside
in memory of her

We will bring what is costly
in memory of her

We will break open our gifts
in memory of her

We will fill the house with our fragrance
in memory of her

We will claim our prophetic powers
in memory of her

We will anoint the body
in memory of her

We will insist on saying our names
in memory of her

We will retell her story, as we make our own
in memory of her

The anointing

for Ramona

She watches practised hands
mix oils from glass vials and bottles,
sniffing their aromatic fragrances:
chamomile, rose, geranium, lavender, thyme.
Waits, in anticipation, for the healing work to begin.
Always, even while she's expecting it,
the first contact is a frisson, electric charge of cool hand
on warm skin.
               Her body rises to the touch,
sensation spreads out in all directions along the line
of her limbs. Her mind, chattering monkey in the tree,
gradually desists from its frantic antics – look at me! look
    at me!
settles down to sleep.
               The working hands go deeper,
seeking the places of tension and resistance:
taking the muscle and rolling it, releasing tautness and pain
from trapped pockets of flesh. She breathes deeply into the
    action,
receiving into her naked body
what the hands have to give.
               It is an exchange of sorts.
Bringing her body, all trust, asking mutely
for healing, she must hold nothing back so that she may
    receive
the offering of touch,
the masseur's open heart,
the generous pouring.

Christa gives a mud wrap

Cover me with your love like mud, girl
Pack the hot, brown stuff firm in your
    practised hands
rich with earth's vital energies
and ladle it onto my body –
white, cool, longing for your touch
Smooth me all over with mud
running your fingers quickly up my flesh
Wrap me in cling film, sealing the goodness in
Lay me down on white towels
cover me over with towels
then slowly, expertly, massage my feet
Leave me for a while
to drift in the warm cocooned space
        inside the room
        inside the towels
        inside the river's mud
working its cleansing powers

Put me under the shower
and flannel me down
water dousing my body
making the mud sticky and runny like toffee
Don't stay outside
come in with me   naked
slapping the mud everywhere
laughing as it runs down legs, breasts, arms
two river goddesses

Let's stay under for a long time
watching the milky water
slowly thinning   coming clear

Afterwards we'll step out of the shower
towel each other down
sleepy and soft-skinned as newborn kittens

Stepping outside into the dark evening sky
we'll walk lightly
as the first creatures in Eden

Earth to earth
mud to mud

Washing

Maundy Thursday, Noddfa

Not feet, but hands as we sat around the bare wooden table
in the kitchen where we'd assembled after journeys
that brought us from various places to this temporary
    women's shelter
where we'd come for the making of Pasch.

Perhaps we were too embarrassed to peel off socks, handle
    sweating feet;
or perhaps it just seemed too hackneyed, obvious, too much
    of an aping
of what others would be doing all over the world at this hour,
in churches, cathedrals, chapels.

We sought something simpler, ordinary, the stuff of women's
    lives.
We had a candle, but no formal liturgy.
We took it in turns around the table to wash each other's
    hands,
wipe them clean. Perhaps we smeared on oil, spoke some
    words of blessing.

I can't remember, only recall the kitchen, the table, the
    women's bodies,
silence and the sound of water plashing in the plastic bowl,
rubbing of flannel on flesh.
The darkness outside massing, the one candle burning.

Her face

after Melissa Raphael

washed by hands that were always filthy,
nails grimed with ooze from the unspeakable latrines

in water that was never clean –
ersatz coffee, urine, brackish silt

and sometimes, in no water at all
'in love alone'

the face of one woman, a thousand women
never the same, always the same

faces that tried not to let themselves be
noticed (that way death lay)

faces that were long past any
pretence of prettification

erased by mud, malnutrition
the casual swipes and thumps of the guards

and washed, caressed, tenderly traced by
mothers desperate for the work of love

in that place of all loveless places
that end of modernity's railroad

In just such a place, in just such faces
at the fate of just such stinking, tender hands

her face may have lifted itself up
momentarily

to gaze at her own reflection there
shining for an instant

in the sore-speckled, besmirched
visages of the unwashed filthy

washed

The table of women

'Bring it warm!' a voice instructs
Large baskets of bread
and platters of fish
are piled high

The women eat lustily
oil dripping down their chins
hands ripping the yeasty stuff
to mop the juices up

They lie back on couches
their feet washed and perfumed
their skin healthy and tough

They talk as they eat
of paradise imagined
the children fed
Rome resisted and all that is good shared

There is no priest among them
for all are priests
no formal liturgy
for this is the liturgy of life

The bread of life

After she's paid off the credit card
and bought a pair of trainers from the market for Jack
and spared a bit of loose change
for the bloke outside the Co-op down on his luck
and the bus to her mam's and back
and the weekly lotto
there's barely a tenner left for food.
It'll have to be egg sandwiches for lunch again,
on cheap white sliced,
and for tea whatever they're selling off
past its sell-by date.

Her idea of a balanced diet
is what she can manage to carry
in two carrier bags
without one of them splitting.
If she's lucky, her mam'll have saved her
some apples from the allotment
and a cabbage or potatoes.

Sometimes, she'll starve herself for a day or two
and make the lad do with scanty suppers
so she can blow it all on fish and chips
drenched in salt and vinegar.
They stand in the doorway together,
Jack grinning in spite of himself,
letting the steam warm their bodies through.

At night she dreams of an old-fashioned roast dinner
she'll cook for them both at the weekend –
and tell him to bring his mates along too.
All the trimmings, the way her nan used to make it.
Crumble and custard to follow. As much
to eat as everyone wants. Plenty
left over for the next day, too.
She wakes with the taste of sweet butter in her mouth.

A litany for messy eaters

For Catherine, who can't eat the bread because it will make
 her sick

For Desmond, who won't touch the wine because he's alcoholic

For Rachel, on an enforced liquid diet of chemicals because
 her bowel is packing up

For Grace, who must eat little and often because she's diabetic

For Michael, who's lost all his teeth to jaw cancer and must be
 fed like a baby

For Reg, on a low-fat diet to prevent the recurrence of heart
 attack

We who are many are one body
Because we all share in the one bread

For Justin, who buys only from Waitrose and cooks the finest
 recipes

For Audrey, who swears by her microwave and lives on
 bargains from the market

For Jonas, making curry for twenty and inviting in all the
 neighbours

For Sidney, who always eats alone, feeding the leftovers to
 the cat

For the brothers at Glasshampton, consuming in
 companionable ritual silence

For families catching up on the day's gossip over the supper
 table

We who are many are one body
Because we all share in the one bread

For farmers who can't get the price of a decent meal for their
 livestock

For fruit pickers, tea pickers, cockle pickers doing slave labour

For fisherfolk whose stocks have been shrunk by overfishing

For people whose livelihood on the land has been devastated
 by flood or drought

For families and whole communities uprooted from land by
 war and famine

For all who work for policies of fair trade and ethical land use

We who are many are one body
Because we all share in the one bread

For we who stand around this communion table
For those who are too anxious or fearful to come
For those who have walked out in anger
For those who would come but have not heard an invitation
For people of other faiths sharing ritual food with different
    meanings
For all who long to be included at the welcome table

We who are many are one body
Because we all share in the one bread

At the table of Christa

The women do not serve
but are served

The children are not silent
but chatter

The menfolk do not dominate
but co-operate

The animals are not shussed away
but are welcomed

At the table of Christa

There is no seat of honour
for all are honoured

There is no etiquette
except the performance of grace

There is no dress code
except the garments of honesty

There is no fine cuisine
other than the bread of justice

At the table of Christa

There is no talk of betrayal
but only of healing and hopefulness

No money changes hands
but all know themselves rich in receiving

Death is in no one's mind
but only the lust for life

No one needs to command 'Remember'
for no one present can ever forget

Presiding like a woman

This is how we do it:

In boardrooms, working skilfully so that all the voices can be
 heard.
In kitchens, standing over steaming saucepans, following
 recipes passed down by our grandmothers.
At the table, gathering the day's news from children, guests;
 lighting candles, feeding titbits to the cats.
In operating theatres, administering with precision the deadly
 wounds that will heal.
In parliamentary committees and city councils,
trying to find another way of doing business,
wielding power that enables and includes.
In concert halls, at the rostrum, bringing all that unruly
 creativity into one living, breathing music.
In classrooms, warming to our subject, encouraging the slow and
 quick-witted learners, drawing out incipient wisdom.
In gardens, clearing weeds, making space for things to grow,
planning colours in their right times and seasons.
In bedrooms and at waterpools, leaning over the women
 about to give birth,
holding their sweating hands, looking into their eyes, saying
'Yes! Now! Push!'

In our own voices – elegant, educated; rough, untamed;
 stuttering or eloquent;
in all the languages that God gives.
Or sometimes without voice, silently, through gestures:
the nod of the head, lifting of an arm, sway of our bodies,
the way we move around a space.
Sometimes with permission, mostly without.
Recognized for the priests that we are or, mostly, not.
Never alone: always in the company of sisters,
brothers, children, animals who call our gifts into being
and offer their own for the making of something
that includes everyone and yet is beyond us all.

Seated, standing, lying propped up in beds or couches,
from wheelchairs and walking frames,

proud of our bodies, bent with the burdens we've carried all
   these years
or youthful, resilient, reaching after what's yet to come.

In shanty towns, under rickety roofs made out of tarpaulin,
and high-rise council flats in the centre of sprawling cities.
In remote rural monasteries and out of the way retreat
   centres;
in hospitals, prisons and shopping centres,
factories, office blocks and parliamentary corridors;
in women's refuges and hostels for the homeless,
old people's homes and kids' nurseries,
on death row and in the birthing wards:
every place where human lives jostle, mingle, struggle, despair,
   survive.
In the desert cave and the hermit's hidden cleft,
where land and sky and the company of saints are the
   congregation.

This is how we do it:
not really thinking how we do it but doing it;
not naming it for what it is but sometimes, in flashes,
recognizing the nature of what it is we do:
the calling, the gathering, the creating of community,
the naming, the celebrating and lamenting of a people's
   sorrows and joys,
the taking of what human hands have made,
offering it with thanksgiving and blessing,
the breaking, the fracturing of so many hopes and
   expectations,
to discover something unlooked for, new, beyond the
   brokenness;
the sharing of what has been given by others;
the discovering that, even out of little, hungers are fed,
hurts healed, wounds not taken away but transfigured –
the bearing, the manifesting of the body of God,
the carrying in our bodies of the marks of the risen one;
seeing the light reflected in each other's eyes,
seeing Her beauty mirrored in each one's softened face.

The agony

Hers was a struggle
not to let go into death
but the freefall into life.

Stuck in the place of
paralysis, longing for release
into her own powers

the muting of them making her
ill, for years she'd lived
behind walls that hemmed her

in: walls of her own
making, hated yet needed,
walls that only she could

clamber up, leap over and
finally dismantle.
There came an hour

after months and years
of battering against that bloody wall,
flinging all her rage against it to no avail

when she knew of an instant
– utterly incredulous –
it was ready to crumble.

This was the moment of purest terror,
she'd never known fear like it.
She had to go way down inside herself

to find the courage to face
the terror one last time.
She couldn't see, she was caught

in the paws of some terrified
animal, suffocating
against its foul breath.

She screamed against it, sweat
and blood in her eyes, though
her mouth felt gagged. Some

ministering angel
held her to it, kept her nerve.
Just when she felt

she must pass out, be swallowed
alive, succumb for ever to its jaws,
she felt herself forced up on her legs,

staggering upright
to see the creature bound off,
herself staring at a gaping hole

where the wall had always stood.
Stones and bricks
scattered at her feet, a haze of dust,

a vista such as she'd never imagined.
This was the moment for
gathering all her courage

in both hands, for picking up the cup
of life, shining at her feet,
and draining it, full,

in one gulp. This was the moment
of assent to her own free will,
without stint or measure,

for shaking off any last vestige of fear
or sacrificial gesture.
This was the moment of Yes.

Passiontide sequence

Eucharist

Love sparkled in our guests' eyes,
in the champagne glasses and our sequined silks.
Sun spilled over the lawns and the tables.
Our joy knew no bounds.
We couldn't guess it then, but the wedding banquet was our
    last supper.

Betrayal

Was it your body that betrayed you, hiding its secret?
Or the surgeon, less of a demi-god than he, and we, wanted
    to think?
Was it the unerringly inefficient NHS machine?
Or, God forgive, was it me,
who didn't realize how bad things had gotten,
didn't rush you back to hospital sooner,
didn't make a big enough fuss,
didn't insist on immediate and urgent action?

Gethsemane

You couldn't sleep at night.
Your body was agitated, fretful.
Imperceptibly at first, and then with alarming speed,
you puffed up, your belly twice its normal size.
When the doctors drained it off, you were in agony.
I had to leave, couldn't bear to stand by and hear you
    shouting.
Later, you reacted badly to the dye they squirted into your
    abdomen.
You were doped up with morphine
but it wasn't touching the pain.
Next day, you couldn't lift your head or speak to me.
You went somewhere far, far away and
how could anyone blame you?
I left, weeping my way up the long corridor
all the way home in the car
and into the solitary bed.

Foot-washing

I lifted the blue plastic bowl from behind your bed,
filled it with warm water from the small ward sink,
fragranced it with lavender.
With an exaggerated gentleness,
I soaped your face, arms and hands,
your legs and feet.
I kissed your brow,
wetting your cheeks with my tears.
You lay back on the pillows, smiled at me weakly.

Procession

Alone, I tramped the corridor to West 1 several times a day,
from Metchley Lane and back again,
to and from the car,
taking away rubbish and dirty washing,
bringing in clean things.
Friends appeared and disappeared in ones and twos,
carrying cards, flowers, fruit – the usual offerings.
Hospital staff made their ceaseless forays.
Even at night, the procession never faltered,
just slowed a little:
monitoring, measuring, adjusting, assessing.

The watch

Sitting by your bed while you doze or sleep.
Holding your hand lightly, when you can bear my touch.
Feeling the deprivation when you can't.
Reading the cards that have arrived.
Counting the hours between drug rounds.
Watching the pain in your face lessen or intensify,
your body stiffen against the next procedure.
Seeing the shock on people's faces,
arming myself against their concern.
Waiting for test results,
for the surgeon to tell us his plan,
for a space in theatre.
Counting the days for you to come home again, uncertain.

The body of Christa

Desert canyon, harsh, unyielding
Night sky over the bush
Icy rivers moaning on their way to the sea
Forests denuded and replanted
Oceans warming and flooding low-lying islands
Volcanoes, geysers, thermal landscapes
of grotesque, unearthly appearance
(all the colours in God's palette shining or absorbing)
Snowdrops half-submerged in ice in an English monastery
    garden
Craggy mountain passes
enormous mesas, wide open to the sky
Fog on flat fenlands
Curlews crying across Suffolk mudflats

This is the body of Christa
given for us

Take, eat
flesh of the world preserve our own bodies and souls
unto everlasting life

After the mass is ended we go
our bodies imprinted on her mutable beauty

A litany for Passiontide

On the suffering body of Christa
teach us to show mercy

On the bleeding body of the earth
teach us to show mercy

On the denuded forests and blighted trees
teach us to show mercy

On the polluted rivers and the over-farmed oceans
teach us to show mercy

On the low-lying islands and unprotected coasts
teach us to show mercy

On the deforested lands and the eroded soil
teach us to show mercy

On the endangered species of bird, plant, animal and insect
teach us to show mercy

On the ever-expanding cities and the dwindling wilderness
teach us to show mercy

On the carbon-filled airways and congested roads
teach us to show mercy

On our own harassed, over-stimulated, burdened bodies
teach us to show mercy

On the bodies of the poor, the homeless and the destitute
teach us to show mercy

On the body politic in our own land and throughout
   the world
teach us to show mercy

That we may companion the wounded Christa
good Spirit, strengthen us

That we may comfort her anguish
good Spirit, strengthen us

That we may stand with her sorrow
good Spirit, strengthen us

That we may help bear her burden
good Spirit, strengthen us

That we may share in her labour
good Spirit, strengthen us

Until the whole creation is delivered from its birthpangs
and her children are set free from bondage

4

Christa crucified

Good Friday

Of all days of the liturgical year, Good Friday must rank as the most solemn, intense and demanding – perhaps akin in its weight and significance to the Jewish Day of Atonement, Yom Kippur, for observant Jews. This is the day on which Christians recall the death of Christ and his agony both leading up to the cross and on the cross itself; and not only 'recall' it, as if watching or rehearsing some historical drama of the past, but actively seek to enter into it, to participate in the Passion of the Lord and, insofar as one may, to share in it – to walk the way of the cross with Jesus, to remain standing with him as he dies on the cross, to pray with and into his suffering. Traditionally, this day is regarded as a day of fasting, penance and silence (although in some Protestant traditions, there is an emphasis on joy and victory at the accomplishment of salvation achieved in the cross). In many denominations, the Three Hours from noon to three in the afternoon are kept as a period of observance, marking the time when Jesus is thought to have suffered on the cross, before his death.

There are many variations around the world in the way this day is marked and ritualized – including Good Friday walks of witness and processions (with or without a cross), the traditional Stations of the Cross, veneration of the cross, as well as services combining addresses, prayers, music, silence and so on. In some traditions, it is customary to refrain from receiving communion on Good Friday (so that the Eucharist is not celebrated between Maundy Thursday and the first Eucharist of Easter), while in other traditions the Eucharist marks the climax of the Good Friday Three Hours liturgy – although generally shorn of many of its regular features. Different Christian traditions of observance call attention to different aspects of Christ's death, often representing strongly contrasting theologies.

Feminist theologians, among others, have expressed a good deal of ambivalence toward, if not outright repudiation of, the centrality of the cross in Christian thinking, worship and ethics, and feminists are therefore among those who may feel a good deal of tension and uncertainty about Good Friday itself, and about the most appropriate ways to mark this day – or even whether it should be marked out in any special way at all. I share that ambivalence, as each year, I find myself in church, fixing my attention and prayer for some three hours on the horrible death of a man two thousand years ago – wondering what on earth I'm doing there, yet finding it impossible to imagine being anywhere other than in church. I am both drawn to and repelled by the cross, my mind full of nagging questions, yet carrying a sense that it is important to be here, with other Christians, marking this day; that we need to be here, that we are doing something that is significant, even essential – even if I'm not quite sure exactly what it is I think we *are* doing and what are the most helpful ways of understanding the theological significance of the death of Christ. It is worth reminding ourselves that the earliest Christian creeds never defined doctrine around the death of Christ too closely. 'Christ died for our sins', the creeds proclaim, but they don't spell out what that means or commit believers to any one particular model or theory of atonement.

The questions which feminists and others have raised around the cross are multiple. Is the cross essential to the gospel or could we envisage an alternative ending to the life of Jesus which did not culminate in violent death (as one of my poems, later in this chapter, attempts)? Does an exclusive focus on the suffering and death of Jesus somehow cancel out or nullify women's bodily and spiritual sufferings, deflecting attention from the bodies that cry out for care and healing in our own world? Or, on the contrary, is it the most profound symbol and expression of human (including female) suffering that we can imagine and does it, rightly understood, capture up all those other deaths, symbolically 'hold' them and compel a response to suffering wherever it is found? Is the veneration of the cross an unspeakable act of complicity with systems of torture and violence, and an identification of God with the powers of destruction in the world, or is it, conversely, to challenge and subvert those very powers? And how are we to understand the work of God in the cross, if we indeed believe that the cross is part of God's salvific work? If we speak of 'atonement', what do we mean by that, and what meanings are appropriate and liberative for our time? Are notions of sacrificial offering, for instance, irredeemably patriarchal, serving only to sanction the sacrificial suffering of women, children and the poor and oppressed in the world today, deserving no place in a contemporary feminist theology, or can notions of sacrifice have anything useful to say to women's lives? If we speak of the shed blood and broken body of Christ as redemptive, what does that have to say to the life-giving blood of women and the bodies of women who bear life, through agony, in the world?

These are just some of the questions which have been addressed by feminist theologians, and which have major implications for the liturgical celebration of Good Friday. I first became aware of such questions a good while ago now, but one particular Holy Week, when I was staying at Malling Abbey and reading a range of texts raising such questions, became a catalyst and a focus for me to wrestle with them with particular urgency (see the journal extract below). Feminist liturgists, according to their response to such questions, have taken a number of different approaches to the ritualization of Good Friday. Some have focused, not only or primarily on the suffering and death of Jesus, but upon the faithfulness and witness of the small group of women who remained with Jesus at his death, refusing to abandon him (as most of the male disciples did), thereby shifting the centre of Good Friday from the death on the cross to the birth of life and hope on that day. Others want to call attention to the shed blood and broken bodies of women and children throughout history and in our world today, as expressions of the Passion of Christ, and as sites of God's creative and redemptive work. Others, again, proclaim the cross as God's ultimate protest against all unjust suffering and as the final act of divine suffering which puts an end to any other crosses in the lives of women and men in the world. The cross of Christ is seen as the last cross, not to be repeated, emulated or adored. Or the cross is seen, not so much as a symbol of death and violence, but as the paradoxical symbol of holism and healing, the archetypal tree of life which reconciles earth and heaven, which reunites vertical and horizontal axes in a symbol of inclusion, balance and fruitfulness. To venerate such a cross will mean something very different from the elevation of an instrument of torture as God's chosen means of salvation.

The figure of the Christa, who has been most often depicted as a crucified, dying figure, is, of course, another key way in which artists, liturgists and theologians have responded to the cross and to women's suffering. The Christa has many meanings, but a dominant one for many women seems to be the proclamation of women's bodily and other kinds of suffering as worthy of recognition, honour and symbolic representation, to stand alongside the thousands of images of male suffering and of the male Christ. The image of the suffering Christa compels the viewer to gaze on women's bodies as sites of violent abuse and oppression, to recognize and remember the countless women and girls whose bodies are exploited, battered, raped and killed – and to recognize that these are the pains of a God who suffers and dies with every woman abused, raped, maimed and dismembered. Even though, in this book, I am seeking to broaden reflection on the Christa away from an exclusive focus on the crucified female figure, I cannot ignore the power of this figure and its potential to speak to suffering women, and to men who wish to respond to women's pain – nor would I want to.

At Noddfa, we did not have the time or inclination to engage all these potential issues, but we did want to open at least some of them up for exploration and reflection. We wanted to find a way of marking Good Friday that was authentic, creative, informed by feminist debate, rooted in our own lives and experience, respectful of our own place and time, yet also attentive to our various Christian traditions and to the gospel narrative of Jesus' own journey to the cross. In the morning, we took time together as a group to reflect on our own experiences of the cross, however we interpreted that, seeking to honour pain and crucifixion in our own lives and the lives of those close to us. We asked ourselves the question: where and who is the crucified Christa in our midst? Women spoke about many different kinds of suffering, their own and others': violence and abuse, whether physical, sexual, verbal or other kinds; broken or dysfunctional relationships; physical pain and illness; mental and psychological stigma and suffering; rejection, betrayal and loneliness; failure to have one's vocation recognized or affirmed; the refusal of love; discrimination on the basis of gender, sexuality or class; the loss through death or other means of a child, a partner, a close friend; and so on. We pondered on the place such suffering had played in our lives, trying to be honest about whether we could see anything creative or redemptive in our own suffering (many of us could), or whether, in some instances, pain had been apparently wholly destructive, something we needed actively to resist and name as evil.

Out of our sharing and reflection, we moved towards the construction of our Good Friday liturgy. We decided that this was to take the form of a traditional Stations of the Cross, in which we would remember the suffering of Jesus but widen reference out to include our own sufferings and those of other women, men and children, using our own words and experiences to invest the traditional format with new meaning. In twos and threes, we took responsibility for preparing a series of 'stations'. At noon, we began our procession, in silence, out of the retreat house gardens onto the Jubilee Path that winds round a large, grassy hill to the rear of the retreat house. We carried a cross roughly constructed out of large branches, and, at various points along the way, according to the instinct of the group, stopped for each station. The first stop was for the women of Jerusalem, and for women around the world today who bear the sufferings of their communities. We stood in silence, speaking aloud or silently in our hearts the names of communities and women we wanted to recall, standing in solidarity with them. The next stop was entitled 'splitting the stone', and was an expression of the pain we may experience at being apart from those we love, the pain of any community that is experiencing some kind of split or wound. We were invited to take a stone from the path and bash it, hard, against another rock; to feel our own anger, despair and hurt. The third stop was for children who suffer; we collected stones for children we knew who were in pain of different sorts, and built a small cairn, naming the children's names as we laid them. The next station was for 'carrying burdens', and we recalled our own burdens and those of others of whom we were conscious. We were invited to let go of a burden and leave it on the hillside. So with these and other stations, we continued to travel up the hill, until we arrived at a small cave burrowed into the side of the hill, where we built a final cairn of stones and placed the cross of branches we had carried up the hill. We tied ribbons to the branches, as an expression of our own identification with the pain and the victory of the cross. Then we left the makeshift cross and made our own ways, in silence, back down the hill.

This rather roughshod Good Friday liturgy represents, of course, only one, provisional and partial, attempt to respond creatively to the challenge of creating authentic feminist liturgy around pain, suffering and death – and I would not want to claim too much for it. It is one example among many. During the course of working on this book, I also had the experience of being involved in a more traditional liturgical Good Friday 'Three Hours', when I was invited to give the addresses at St James, Piccadilly. Although the format of the service was recognizably and classically Anglican, the whole experience took on a new and radical edge when, in consultation with the clergy and lay leaders at St James, I decided to focus the addresses on the figure of the Christa. Prayers, hymnody, dance and visual imagery were all chosen to complement this focus, so that old and new, well-known traditions and fresh expressions of faith, were placed alongside each other in startling and challenging ways to illuminate the Passion of God in the experiences of women, girls, and others of the marginalized, including the ravaged earth itself. Some of the material that follows came out of this Good Friday experience.

Wrestling with the cross: journal extract
Good Friday 2000, Malling Abbey

1

What am I – what are we all – doing in this place over these 'holy days'? What is the meaning of this commemoration of the betrayal, suffering and death of Jesus? What am I participating in? What theological and psychological truths am I assenting to? What political and institutional systems of power am I giving credence to?

I find myself deeply disturbed and distressed this Holy Week by feminist challenges to traditional understandings of the death of Christ and to key liturgical practices of the Eucharist and the rites of the Triduum. I'm reading Marjorie Procter-Smith's *Praying with Our Eyes Open*, which delivers some hefty charges against Christian public prayer as it has been practised for centuries and critiques in particular the centrality of Christ in Christian prayer, the focus on his death and suffering understood as sacrificial and redemptive, and the Eucharist as a memorial of that redemptive suffering. Procter-Smith's sharp critique is intensified and magnified by the devastating attack on Christian theologies of the cross and atonement levelled by the essayists in *Christianity, Patriarchy and Abuse: A Feminist Critique*, which I'm also reading. Together, these essayists launch a virtually unassailable case against Christianity as a system which has condoned, legitimized and glorified the worst excesses of violence and abuse against women, children and black people, and which has worshipped a male sadist God, a cosmic child abuser, a rapist writ large.

These ideas aren't exactly new, I've long known them. But I haven't focused on them, wrestled with them, addressed them head-on as I'm now being compelled to do. The urgency of this agenda made all the more sharp by a visit yesterday to the magnificent 'Seeing Salvation' exhibition at the National: an exploration of images of Christ in Western art to mark the millennium. Magnificent, but hugely disturbing too. The dominance of images of violence and suffering passively accepted, the fixation on blood and the wounds of Christ, the extraordinary ingenuity brought to bear on the elaboration of Christ's journey to the cross, the multiplication of images of violence, abuse, mutilation, the intense, quasi-erotic fascination with death – all this left me reeling, squirming in pain and confusion, wanting to cry out against such terrible, blasphemous stuff – yet confused, shaken, because such images of Christ on the cross, taken down from the cross and so on, have been powerfully affecting in my own life, have been for me – I have thought – salvific, redemptive, revelatory of the love and grace of God.

But are they? Can they be? How am I to understand this central symbol of Christianity? How am I to stand *here*, in this place – the abbey – at this time, facing toward the cross, in integrity and with 'open eyes', as Marjorie Procter-Smith bids me to do, without consenting to the victimization of women and others who are powerless, without giving allegiance to coercive power, without becoming complicit in a ritual that valorizes suffering, passivity, powerlessness and abuse?

I don't know. I'm confused and uncertain about what I *am* doing here, can only hear these disturbing challenges, live into these unsettling questions, wrestle with these unwelcome thoughts.

2

I want to say that S's [a family friend] death – and dying – is sacred, holy, unique, unrepeatable. I'm not sure I can say it's 'redemptive' or 'salvific', I certainly *don't* want to say it's 'sacrificial'. But it's a 'good death', paradoxically, and deserves the attention, honour, reverence that any human life and death should command.

Does singling out Jesus' death as of unique significance help or hinder in the work of attending to, and caring for, the dying of other human beings? I don't know. If we say Jesus' death is 'unique', unrepeatable, salvific in a way no others are, does that not detract from the meaning and sacredness of other deaths? And how can Jesus' death 'save' me? 'Save' from what? And why is his death 'necessary'? Demanded by whom or what? And why must it be (must it be?) violent, bloody, agonizing in the extreme? Yet there are countless other violent, agonizing deaths of good people now and throughout history (too many) which we don't honour, worship, venerate, barely notice at all. Why single out *his* death? Why make it into an object of adoration, worship, veneration, abstracted from his life, his teaching, all that he was and said and did? And when we do, what happens? We glorify violence, we venerate death, we impute to God a strange, masochistic mentality that then breeds the same blood lust in us, 'his' children.

I feel alien from all this. On a beautiful, quiet spring day when life is in the ascendancy, I have no hunger for blood, I do not want to be with death. Or, if I can't evade the reality of death ever present in and with life, I want to be with death as I was/am with S's death: paying careful respect to the particularity of *his* death, attending to the divine presence in *his* body and sufferings, and in R's ministrations and mute agony, believing God to be as present to *this* particular process of death and dying as he was to the death of Jesus – no more and no less.

Sometimes, the death of Jesus, the symbol of the cross, the Easter Triduum, the Eucharist, can focus and express what is true and real for others, and the world in general, and I have often known it so. But today I feel the force of the arguments which say it's all a distraction from the suffering of the world, it's a slur on the uniqueness and particularity of every suffering and dying, it's an elaborate ritual that lifts us out of the real, distances us from it, abstracts us from the concrete here and now we need to attend to: particular struggling human beings and communities, in all their glory and woundedness, beauty and pain; and the body of the earth, the body politic, the life of the cosmos.

3

What might be a liturgical alternative to the traditional veneration of the cross as we are going to practise it here? One alternative might be to expose, denounce and lament false images and namings of the cross, viz:

Christus Victor, the cross of victory, which denies real suffering and pain and gives rise to a martyrdom complex;

Christ as Victim, the cross of shame, and all images which glorify the pain of Christ, emphasize the humiliation, exaggerate his helplessness and his willingness to be crucified – used against countless numbers of women, children and slaves to encourage acceptance of their suffering;

The cult of the wounds – quasi-pornographic images of the wounds and nails, abstracting and objectifying Christ's suffering, giving them enormous veneration, while denying and dishonouring, repudiating the bodies and sexuality of women;

Arma Christi, the lurid fascination with the instruments of torture, all male fixation with violence and weapons of violence, whether that be weapons of warfare, pornographic fantasies of violence against women or children, or the desire for ever-increasingly powerful machines and cars that drive at excessive speeds that can kill and destroy the planet;

and so on.

Or, a positive veneration of symbols of life, such as plants, foliage, perhaps the Tree of Life image as an alternative way of reading the cross.

Who is the Christa?

Every woman forced to have sex who didn't want it
Every girl trafficked out of her own home country
trapped in some anonymous bedsit in someone else's city
working all the hours men want to have her body

The woman you meet in the street with bruises all up her arm
Every woman who is too frightened to go out alone
because of what has happened to her in the past
or what she imagines might happen to her

The woman sleeping in the underpass
in her makeshift room of cardboard
who wards off the unwanted attentions from the drunk two
    streets up

The smart young graduate climbing the career ladder
who can't get through the day without shooting up
The anorexic teenager starving her young body
that is strange to her and she cannot seem to love
The classrooms of self-harming girls

The nine-year-old orphan caring for three siblings all under
    five
in a shanty town in any African city

Every street girl and boy scavenging on rubbish tips
Every child working in sweatshops making cheap tee-shirts
All the women raped in war or, worse, forced to watch their
    daughters raped
Husbands shot in front of their eyes

Women who walk a thousand miles through a war zone
babies on their hips and children dragging along beside them
Desperate to make it to a refugee camp
where they might find food and shelter

Christa our sister
have mercy
Christa God's beloved
show us your face
where we have not wanted to see it
where we resist your presence among us

Confession for Good Friday

When we have idolized the body on the cross
and ignored our suffering sisters and brothers:
Christa, forgive us

When we have worshipped the symbol of death
and failed to nurture a spirituality of life:
Christa, forgive us

When we have venerated the blood of a dying man
and abhorred the blood of menstruating women:
Christa, forgive us

When we have promoted a theology of sacrifice
and refused a theology of resistance:
Christa, forgive us

When we have wanted to stay in the place of the skull
and resisted your rising in our midst:
Christa, forgive us

Wherever the cross is employed
as a justification of suffering:
Christa, empower us to resist

Wherever the cross is held aloft
as a weapon of warfare:
Christa, empower us to protest

Wherever the cross is paraded
as a symbol of patriarchy:
Christa, empower us to refuse

Wherever the cross is sanctified
with the pomp and privilege of those whose suffering is slight:
Christa, empower us to anger

Give us faith and courage to abandon every form of the cross
which enslaves, oppresses and maims.
Teach us to recognize the true cross
in the lives of those who suffer
and to see your form in our crucified sisters and brothers.
Amen.

Christa sister

Christa sister
have mercy

Christa sister
where are you?

Christa sister
do not forsake me

Christa sister
I cannot see you

Christa sister
do not hide your face from me

Christa sister
show me your beauty

Christa sister
come out of the shadows

Christa sister
show me your wounds

Christa sister
let me find you

Christa sister
have mercy

Christa crucified

It seems we need her dead and dying
to speak to women's graves

We need her bleeding and gasping
to gesture to women's pain

We need her strung up on a cross
to render visible the abuse that's daily in our papers

We need her gagged, maimed and whipped
to gesture towards unspeakable things
that are still done to young girls, adolescents, grown women
   the world over

We need her body spread open, legs apart
to stand for all that has split women open

We need her abject and ashamed
to body forth the contours of women's shame

And I'm still looking for her risen form
somewhere   somehow   someplace

striding towards a new dawn

The concubine's communiqué

Judges 19

My body is a letter.
Consider, take counsel and send your reply.

To Reuben, the left forearm shorn off from shoulder to elbow.
Arm yourselves for war.
What has been done to me will be done to you and more.

To Simeon, one severed breast, wrapped in sackcloth.
Beat your breasts for the crime committed in Gibeah.

To Ephraim, ten bloody fingers.
Everything you have handled shall be destroyed by fire.

People of Zebulun, do not stiffen your necks against
    the coming vengeance.
As mine was broken, so shall yours be.

Tribe of Dan, receive this tongue, torn out to stop my
    screaming.
You shall cry aloud for the mouths of wailing children
    to be gagged,
but your prayer will not be heeded.

To Asher, my right foot still in its silver sandal.
    To Gad, my left.
You shall walk where you do not wish to go
as I was compelled to go where I would not.

Naphtali, gentle as the doe, here are my two eyes
that shall never see again. You will be blinded by
    blood and tears.

To Issachar and Zebulun, one severed ear apiece.
Ear has not heard nor tongue told what has
    befallen me,
and what shall come to you.

To Judah, the empty womb that never gave birth.
Pregnant women in you will not come to term,
nor will the virgins conceive.
Your streets will be silent of children's laughter.

To the people of Manasseh, east and west,
my two strong legs, with their veins still pink.
You shall not stand.

O tribe of Benjamin, do not think yourself favoured.
Your heart that beats for God shall be pierced,
as mine was, and divided into twelve bleeding pieces.

A daughter's prayer of abandonment

My father, my father
Why have you deserted me?

I called to you but you did not answer
I ran to you but you turned away

Father, look on my distress
Tears have been my pillow in the morning and the night

All night long I tossed and turned
Because you have abandoned me

I called to you but you did not answer
I ran to you but you turned away

O my father, I would pour out my heart to you
I would open the book of my life to you so that you might
  read there

When I am in sorrow, would I not tell you?
When my life is overflowing with joy, do I not long for you to
  share it?

I called to you but you did not answer
I ran to you but you turned away

What have I done to you that you will not look on me?
What good have I not done that you will not come to me?

My love is spurned, my joy is rejected
My heart is pierced, my body is broken

I called to you but you did not answer
I ran to you but you turned away

Will you not turn again, that the body you have broken may
  be healed?
Will you not mend your ways, that my crushed spirit may be
  raised?

O my father, have pity on me!
Do not reject a daughter's pleading but come to my aid.

A canticle for Passiontide

based on Isaiah 63

Who is this that comes from Edom,
from Bozrah in garments stained crimson?

It is I, Christa, glorious in my blood-red gown.

Who is this so splendidly robed,
marching in her great might?

It is I, Christa, leading an army of sisters to victory.

Why are your robes red, O daughter of Zion,
and your garments like theirs who tread the wine press?

My robes are red with the blood
that has been hounded out of the sanctuary.

My garments are stained with the menstrual blood
that has been decried and desecrated on the altars.

My vestments are dripping with the blood
of countless stillbirths, abortions and hysterectomies.

My skirts are crimson with the birth blood
of the entire human race.

It is I, Christa, who have trodden the wine press alone,
sweating with the women in labour,
crying out with the girls terrified at the sight of their own
    blood.

Their juice is spattered on my garments,
staining all my robes red.

I cry aloud with their pain and will not cease my lamentation
until their vindication is accomplished.

Pavane pour une enfante défuncte

after Melissa Raphael

Mothers in Auschwitz
sang to the silence

lullabies to their dead children
psalms to their absent god

whose own maternal song
soothed her daughters to sleep

the death of the righteous
by the kiss of the Shekinah

Was she extinguished by violence?
Theologians have said so

but the mothers' covenantal anguish
may tell another tale

of the dying and yet deathless
cleaving Mother love

which even in the holocaustal pit
refuses to unclasp

the deceased, harrowing body
of her own child

A prayer to Mother God

God our Mother, Source of all life,
compassionate and present,
protector of the poor and the marginalized:

Stand with the women and girls of Africa,
especially those infected with HIV and AIDS
yet still caring for the sick and the dying,
working to keep families and communities together:

God our Mother
stand with all who would otherwise fall.

Stand with the women and men of Palestine,
estranged from their land and homesteads,
separated by the wall from their neighbours and
    fields,
restrained, restricted and frustrated in their efforts
    to live ordinary lives:

God our Mother
stand with all who would otherwise fall.

Stand with the women and men of Haiti
working to rebuild their devastated towns and
    villages,
trusting in you for the livelihoods they do not
    possess,
for the stability and hope in short supply:

God our Mother
stand with all who would otherwise fall.

Stand with women and girls in China
emerging from centuries of oppression
to find their freedom and their contribution to
    a new society
yet still facing discrimination, abuse, victimization:

God our Mother
stand with all who would otherwise fall.

Stand with the poorest communities in the West
at a time of recession, shrinkage of employment
    opportunities,
cutbacks to benefits and social security.
Protect the elderly, the sick and children –
those who are most vulnerable when resources
    are scarce.

God our Mother
stand with all who would otherwise fall.

A litany to Christa our friend
John 15.13

We adore you, O Christa, and we bless you
because out of love for your friends,
you freely laid down your life.

Like the midwives who defied the injunction of Pharaoh
and risked their own lives that the newborns might live,
you faced the powers that would crush your own life,
so that you might birth daughters and sons for God.

We adore you, O Christa, and we bless you
because out of love for your friends,
you freely laid down your life.

Like the widow who gave all that she possessed,
even her very livelihood,
you held back not one portion of your life for safe keeping
but freely expended it all:

We adore you, O Christa, and we bless you
because out of love for your friends,
you freely laid down your life.

Like the woman who lavished her love on her beloved,
anointing the body with tears and caressing it with her hair,
you poured out your love on humankind,
not counting insults or reviling:

We adore you, O Christa, and we bless you
because out of love for your friends,
you freely laid down your life.

Like the desperate mother who insisted on healing for her
   daughter,
refusing to give up on her claim,
you have risked rejection and opposition
on behalf of the little ones you love:

We adore you, O Christa, and we bless you
because out of love for your friends,
you freely laid down your life.

Like women and men throughout the ages
who have given themselves in the cause of justice, freedom
    and peace,
you counted your own life less dear
than the prize of the coming kin-dom of God:

We adore you, O Christa, and we bless you
because out of love for your friends,
you freely laid down your life.

Christa victor

Christa, you came as slave:
raped by the white master in the plantations,
whipped by his wife and daughters,
worked to within an inch of your life for another's greed.
Your suffering cried out to heaven.
Your voice, as Sojourner's, rang out in protest and complaint.
You raised up a company of sisters who refused any more to
    be victims.

Christa sister
Christa stranger
Christa victor
Show us our own saving power

Christa, you came as martyr:
snatched in the night by the military
from your village where you worked the fields and taught in the
    classroom,
organized community meetings and led demonstrations.
Taken away to be tortured and killed,
your body bludgeoned and dumped at dawn for the villagers to
    find you,
what you did in life will be remembered
and your bloody death shall not obliterate the memory of your
    saving actions.

Christa sister
Christa stranger
Christa victor
Show us our own saving power

Christa, you came as prophet:
rejected by the ones you sought to serve,
speaking out against every form of social evil,
pitting your energies to withstand the forces that crush.
You endured house arrest, twenty-four-hour police surveillance,
letter bombs, malicious phone calls, parcels filled with excrement.
You refused to be cowed or deflected from your purpose,
pledging your strength in the cause of your people.

Christa sister
Christa stranger
Christa victor
Show us our own saving power

Christa, you came as reconciler:
working in communities divided by generations of conflict,
bringing together those who once would have spat at, or killed,
    each other,
patiently seeking the truth in stories of victim and perpetrator,
bringing to light what has long been hidden,
committing to memory what many preferred to forget.
You showed the way of costly forgiveness,
forged new relationship out of old enmities and embattled
    rivalries.

Christa sister
Christa stranger
Christa victor
Show us our own saving power

Sick Christa

It's not a crucified Christa I need
but a sick one

a Christa lying in bed
with the sheets around her

paralysed not by state machinery or soldiers' rough violence
but by migraine.

Did Jesus ever get sick,
under the weather, menstrual?

How well acquainted was he with depression,
woman's best familiar?

Did he wrestle with the guilt of days and weeks lost to
inertia, lack of confidence, bone-weariness?

Where is the Christa
who will speak to me of this?

I'm not looking for a female replica,
a counterpart of heroic suffering
writ large on a woman's body.
I need another kind of suffering saviour.

I need a Christa who knows about
ME, MS, PMT,
who's been anorexic,
who's binged and thrown up at midnight into the toilet,
who's cut herself
or drunk herself out of misery with a bottle of gin,
or swallowed the cabinet's contents.

I want a Christa who has been there
and come through,
who can talk to me of a woman's salvation
in wounds I can recognize and touch.

Christa, ageing

Say you didn't die a violent death at thirty-three
so we can't immortalize your disfigured but still youthful
    body.
You lived on peaceably enough,
carrying on a trade, getting promotion;
causing a little flurry of controversy from time to time, sure,
with some provocative public statement or other,
but later, once the fuss has all died down,
hitching up with a partner (either sex),
getting yourself a mortgage,
bringing in the money to put the kids through school,
enjoy some decent holidays,
moving to a bigger house once you've retired.
You'd be acquainted with the usual griefs and sorrows:
rheumatism, backache, hot flushes,
joints that start to cause trouble
and bones that need replacing.

Growing older and older,
year collapsing into year,
gradually losing all your friends, one by one,
outliving them all. Partner too.
So you find yourself in your seventies
learning to live alone for the first time,
padding about the empty house at night
in your dressing gown and slippers, talking to the cat.

Imagine yourself looking in the mirror as you clean your
    teeth,
startled at the old woman's face you see there,
fleshy in places where your mother's is,
hair much thinner than it should be,
greying along the edges despite the colour you pay an
    astronomical amount
for the hairdresser to apply.
Tell me you see god in your eyes looking back at you then.

Tree of life
after Lucy d'Souza's painting of the same

And you are a tree of life
roots digging down deep into the fiery heart of the cosmos
branches stretching out to envelop the whole sky

On your body grow the healing leaves
that salve the wounds of the nations
The fruits of the Spirit glisten on your boughs

We draw near and find shelter under your
towering, gnarled limbs:
      rest for our weariness
      shade for our over-heated passions
      cool dark for our over-stimulated senses

Your trunk bears up the weight of the world's sorrowing
      struck by lightning
      lashed by storms and rains
      eaten by insect and worm
      pruned, sawn and ravaged by humans

Still you stand, resplendent in your ageless beauty
glorious in the apparel of each season

There is room for all in your girth
you reject none
spider and beetle
bird and cat
antelope and zebra
hunter and hunted find shelter here
wise one and fool

Good and evil alike may eat of your fruit
You do not judge
absorbing the toxins of our maliciousness
converting them into goodness
offering the juice of your loveliness for our renewal
and pleasure

For you are a tree of life
and we come to you seeking a home

5

The feminist gap

Holy Saturday

Holy Saturday is a strange day, one of the strangest in the entire liturgical calendar, perhaps: a kind of non-day, a non-event, a liminal gap in which very little happens and yet which is absolutely crucial as a space to make the transition from Good Friday to Easter Day. It is a day which often receives very little attention theologically or liturgically (although there are one or two notable exceptions), and yet it is pivotal in the whole experience of Passiontide, fraught with enormous psychological, spiritual and theological significance. Christ is dead and there is nothing to do but slump, with the exhausted disciples, in the dejection of death, hunker down and wait for what is to come. The liturgy on Holy Saturday is shorn down to an absolute minimum: morning and evening prayer, denuded of the usual opening and closing formulas, antiphons and responses, pared down to the knuckle: psalms, without the Gloria; readings, the collect and Lord's Prayer. No bells are rung to announce the start of the offices, the ritual space remains empty of all adornment. In contrast to the intensity of Good Friday, this is a day of recovery, on the one hand, and anticipation on the other, as participants absorb the immensity of what has happened and begin all the practical preparations for Easter (decorating the church, preparing food for the feast). As after any death, the time is marked out with a strange combination of yawning emptiness, numbing fatigue and an enormous amount to do.

Holy Saturday is only a day, a mere twenty-four hours or so, although within the rhythm of the Triduum it is a significant stretch of time, beginning at the end of the Three Hours on Good Friday and extending to the Easter Vigil, whenever that is observed. Symbolically, it represents times in our lives, both as individuals and communities, when we stand in that in-between, liminal space between death and life, after the breakdown or loss of what is most precious to us and before anything new emerges out of death. For feminists, for women in quest of their own identity, selfhood and power as well as new forms of the sacred, I believe Holy Saturday is a space of immense symbolic potential and significance. It can represent for women a psychological space, a gap, a fissure in time, a place of unknowing, waiting, paralysis perhaps, as we move out of one reality into another. In my research into women's faith lives and spiritual journeys, as well as in my own personal journey, I have found this pattern or theme recurring in many different guises as women wrestle with times in their lives of shedding one reality in order to discover something new. Yet movement from one phase, stage or reality to another is hardly ever straightforward or incremental; there is almost always a period or state, sometimes quite prolonged, of being in what William Bridges describes as the 'neutral zone', the in-between space of transition in which all that was once familiar has gone and nothing has yet emerged to take its place. This can be a space characterized by silence and apophatic spirituality, in which language and thought-forms are absent to describe what is going on. It can be a space which is experienced as terrifying or as numbing, as disorienting and excruciatingly lonely, as bewildering or as potentially liberating. Like the desert, this space can be dangerous but it can also manifest its own alluring beauty.

I have used the metaphor, in this chapter, of 'the feminist gap', a space in women's lives which may be experienced in quite a wide range of ways. It may be felt as a space of torpor, paralysis, waiting, struggle, shedding, loss, unknowing, in which women struggle to shake off debilitating forces that silence or oppress, in which we wrestle with the forces of fear and death to birth our own lives, in which we mourn the losses and death of our own powers, our regrets and unfulfilled potential. Yet 'the feminist gap' may also manifest rather more gently and kindly, as the place of rest, sleep, letting go, sinking down, acceptance and recovery. It is the gap we experience daily in the rhythm of waking and sleeping when, at night, we close off from our conscious state, and sink into a state of unconsciousness – a time when nothing apparently is going on, and yet which is essential for human well-being and creativity. It is the gap in between creative productivity which every artist, writer and thinker knows: when we put the pen down (or switch off the laptop), when we finish one poem or chapter or project, and before the next one is birthed, when we set the work aside for a time and go for a walk, or a sleep, or to do the dishes. For years I used to think that such times were interruptions to the work, and I would variously feel guilty for taking 'time off', anxious that the creativity might not return or resentful of those who didn't appear to experience such stops and starts. Now I have come to see them as essential parts of the process of creativity – not apart *from* the process, but a part *of* it, integral to the work and a witness to the mysterious, graced nature of the creative act. Paradoxically, it is when one lets go of conscious control, in rest or sleep or play, having done what work one can, that the unconscious does its own work, and it is often out of such gaps that the next idea or sentence or image is given.

At Noddfa, we tried to keep Holy Saturday as empty as possible, in order to give time and space for reflection on the previous day and for silence, rest and recovery; yet there was also necessary preparation time as we looked ahead to Easter morning and worked on the liturgy for Easter Day as well as making preparations for feasting and partying. After an empty morning, we gathered to share something of our own experiences of 'being in the tomb', paying attention to the gap of Holy Saturday itself, before thinking about how we wanted to mark Easter Day and move into a celebration of new life.

In what follows, there are pieces drawn from various times in my life in which I have experienced Holy Saturday liminal gaps, in a wide variety of moods and guises, as well as reflections on this 'gap' as I've observed it in other women's lives.

The Christa of Holy Saturday

She's been under the sheets for days
refusing to get up

She's not interested in food or sex
or seeing friends

She turns her face from the light
she doesn't want to think about clothes
or concerts or what she's meant to be doing

She wants to rip the pages of her diary out
She wants to cancel it all
She wants everyone to go away

She wants to stay here on her bed
listening to the rain gurgling down the gutters
the liquid song of the birds

let the green of the trees outside her window
comfort her

She wants to weep
if only weeping would come
and sleep for ever

She wants nobody to disturb her
asking for some miracle
that she should answer the phone
or plan the rest of her life

She wants to be raised
She doesn't want to be raised
Don't rouse her

She wants to rest in her tomb
let no one move the stone for a month or two

She is the salvation that cannot be hastened
the cure I need to know sick before she will heal me

She is the woman in the grave
who won't be raised
until she will raise me

The women of unholy Saturday

We are the women who prefer our graves
We are the women who will not be raised

We are the ones who need to be contained
We are the women who choose our restraints

We remain in our locked rooms
cherishing our bonds

You may call to us and cry to us, shouting our names
We can hear you but we dare not respond

We fear our own dreams
We resist our desires

We need to hide away
We prefer the half light

We are the women who look but cannot be seen
listen but cannot be heard

Do not speak to us of resurrection
We roll our own stones over the mouths of our tombs

The art of sleep

Lying down, giving in
to drowsiness, the heaviness of the body
in fatigue. Birds sing
through the tired mind.
Sunlight plays on closed eyelids.
The heart rests, drifting.

A lifetime is only just time enough
to learn to lay down,
to practise napping as cats do,
to lie as gently on the bed
as stones rest at ease in a river,
as fruit ripens patiently in the bowl.

The carer's litany of waiting

For Rosie

Waiting half an hour when the last lot of drugs have worn off
but it's not time for the next round
knowing I can't stop the pain for one second

Waiting, all our questions ready, for the surgeon
never knowing when he'll appear
Five minutes at your bed if we're lucky
at least a dozen more questions after he's gone
that must wait for tomorrow's rounds
Waiting for test results
the next X-ray, scan, consultation, a clear diagnosis

Waiting for you to come back home
to be well enough to sleep in your own bed
Waiting to be able to touch you and hold you and caress you
without your body flinching
Waiting for the tubes and drains and bags to be removed –
        catheter, nephrostomy, wound drain

Waiting for you to smile again
to put the one and a half stone you've lost back on
sit and move without having to hold your body stiffly in self-
    protection

Waiting for someone to tell us it's all over
everything's all right   you are going to be well

Waiting for the phone to stop ringing
for the time when no one will think
to ask how you are, how I'm coping
look at me with that tender pity
that makes me want to cry and rage and hide and crumble
    and fall down on my knees
and yell 'Can we have our life back now please?'

By the healing pool

John 5.1–9

I am sitting by the healing pool
watching the others go in and out
I need strong arms to lift me up
take me down
where the hot mud spurts and bubbles
place my body
foursquare in the murky waters
feel its heat seep up every inch of my flesh
feel its power work on my limbs
feel its astringent softness cleanse my skin

Christa, come and carry me to your healing waters

Lullaby

I lay me down to rest
I lay me down to wash
I lay me down to fast

Bird will carry me
Breath will carry me
Bed will carry me

In my boat of stone
In my boat of pain
In my boat of sleep

All alone on the ocean
All alone on the deep
All alone in the dark

I lay me down to sleep
I lay me down to die
I lay me down to rest

Wrapping the bones

for Lucy

wrapping the bones
grief found a home

under the tree
earth received her blood

into the wind
words from the void
letting her go

making the flags
here in this place
none of us knew
writing the wounds

waiting the years
walking the past
voicing her gagged cries
praying her bones

spreading the flags
where wind will take them
till fabric frays
    flies to the skies

into the wind
words from the void
letting her go

Green grave

O lay me to rest in the sweet grass
and cover me with ivy.
Let my bed be of springy moss
and lichen grow stealthily over me.

Let the wild things move and live in me:
ant, spider, beetle, mouse.
Let the sparrows build their nests in me
under the trailing greenery.

O never let them guess at me:
who I was, what century I lived in,
how many were my offspring,
my lineage and pedigree.

Let my grave be a bed of tangled leaves.
Let children scamper over me.
Let the sun not pierce its fine tracery
of dank and darkened verdancy.

O cover me with ivy
and never guess that death is here.

How many hours?

How many hours can a dead woman sleep?
She can do days, nights, whole weeks of it
floating on the ocean floor,
hovering over the blind deeps.
Her eyes are open but they do not move.
Her ears receive the ebb and flow of tides
and faint stirrings of a world above.
She remembers the sounds of birdsong,
the scent of bluebells in the woods,
the cry of the owl at night,
the way she remembers her childhood.
These things are real, she has no doubt of that,
but they are far away.
She does not remember how to get there.

The trick is to lie still without volition,
without stirring the dead mind,
let the tides pass over the unseeing eyes,
frond-furling hair drifting this way and that.
Watch the little fishes darting in and out of her open mouth,
flicking their jets of coloured light into her dark locks.

How many days will she lie there inert on the ocean bed
trapped by the weight of her pale flesh?

But after three days (or is it weeks, months, years?)
the ocean floor will shift,
subject to its own mysterious tides,
and her great lumbering body,
huge and bloated, ghostly and pale,
will loosen itself from its moorings and slowly rise, with
    dolphin grace,
float to the surface of her dreamings,
break the molten drift of the waters,
dripping dazzling   with fire.

Woman settling into her sabbatical: journal extract
June 2009, Vaughan Park, New Zealand

'Days aren't long but moments are' says May Sarton in her poem, 'On the gift of being given time' – but perhaps today, both the moment *and* the day are long, an opening out of time as I take the time, savour the time, simply to be here, sit in this place, not going anywhere, not doing anything: a coming to rest that has, I realize, eluded me until now.

It's Saturday early afternoon. I'm sitting outside in the grounds of the retreat centre in one of the many seating areas overlooking the bay, sun pouring over me. There's a group here, but they're all inside getting on with their own things, ignoring me. And the usual week-day staff aren't around.

So what was it I was hoping for in coming here? Precisely this: this beauty, this spaciousness, the sight and sound of the sea surrounding me morning, noon and night. A rhythm of waking and sleeping, praying in that upturned boat of a chapel, open to sea and sky. Time to read and pore over books and nourish my soul. The stirring of creativity, the flexing of the writing hand, the thinking heart. All this has been given me. And the one thing that makes it real or not, that enables the gift not simply to be given but *received*, realized – myself, alive and present to it all.

Perhaps I am slowly, slowly waking, becoming present. I don't know. There are layers and layers of unpeeling to be accomplished, sloughing off of the dead skins. I thought I knew about fatigue. God knows, I've supped at this particular table often enough. But I discover there is a new kind of fatigue I haven't, until now, tasted. There is a fatigue beyond the fatigue of collapse, when I am forced onto my bed for days at a time. There is a more invidious, probably far more common form of exhaustion, when the will keeps the body upright, coping, functioning, doing all the normal things – eating, sleeping, working, shopping, talking, teaching, being at meetings, going to church, answering emails, watching TV, praying, reading – but the heart has shut off, the heart has come to an end of its capacity for feeling, has decided to shut down. The body longs to rest and to cry but it can't; it has disassociated from whatever centre it once had. The soul has gone somewhere on holiday, some place far far away, and doesn't know how to come back.

This is a fatigue that doesn't manifest in the usual symptoms: lack of energy, long hours of lying around on the bed, a torpor that fills up the body. Rather, there is an inability to rest, both internally and externally. The flesh can look healthy, tanned – as mine is now. The taut lines in the face can relax, one can sleep well at night and rise knowing one has rested. But it takes a long, long while for that dried out husk of a person inside to begin to heal, to soak up the sweet rain and dew of the earth, to take nutrients into itself and store them there so that, in time, it will be ready to send out roots and put up shoots, and grow back into the world again.

For a long time, it will look as if nothing is happening. I rise each day, I pray, I sit reading, I even write a little. And still, I am a long way away. I am not fully present to any of it, except in tiny fits and starts, the odd crack in that old shrivelled vessel, the heart, a sudden, alarming shaft of feeling. I watch two women embrace lovingly during the peace at church and quite suddenly, my eyes fill with tears. I trudge along the beach thinking and seeing nothing; a shift in the quality of light (which happens here all the time) sets the sea shimmering and I feel a stirring of some long lost desire, a resemblance to some feeling I once knew agitating my body. Mostly, I just carry on: reading, taking notes, praying the office, smiling at people, responding as if I am interested when they speak to me (I am, of course I am – don't think me impolite), eating the copious good food they prepare for me. Walking the beach morning and evening, in all weathers.

I do not ask what any of this means. I do not ask why I needed to cross the world to do these simple, ordinary things in some other people's land that is thousands of miles from my own, in a season that is not my body's natural season, in a light that is strange and new and beautiful, far from the places and the plants and the faces I love.

I watch myself, a middle-aged Englishwoman far from home in this beautiful place where everything she could need has been provided, at the start of her sabbatical: fatigued yet unable to name her distress, unable even, yet, to feel her distance from all that is life and home and source to her; only gradually, imperceptibly yielding to the rhythms of a gentler life: feeling the hand of sun caressing her cheek each day, wind lifting her hair, light cascading in waves over the dead skin of her flaking pores. Without realizing it, she is softening to the sound of the sibilant sea, she is moving into the rhythm of the land's pauses and silences, its growing darkness. She may soon begin to murmur in her dreams and dream of what she, as yet, cannot remember or, remembering, name.

This is the way a woman's grief may be held in the palm of a strange land and, over many weeks, be turned, this way and that, left out in the sun and rain, tighten in autumnal cold, expand in the forgiving sun, lie forgotten in some out of the way shadow of the island and, gradually, heal.

This is the way a woman may rise.

6

Christa rising

Easter

Easter is celebrated in a huge variety of forms and ways around the world, but over recent decades there has been a rediscovery of some of the earliest patterns of Christian practice in many of the major denominations worldwide. The great Easter liturgy, as celebrated by Catholic, Orthodox, Anglican and many Reformed traditions, begins with the Easter Vigil, variously kept on the evening of Holy Saturday, through the night or very early, before dawn on Easter Day itself. The unfolding drama of salvation history is narrated with a sequence of readings from the Scriptures which tell of key episodes in the Judaeo-Christian story, interspersed with psalms. Then follows the service of light, playing on the imagery of Christ's resurrection as a light blazing into darkness. The paschal candle is lit, usually from a fire somewhere outside the church building, and processed into the darkened church, with the repeated acclamation 'The light of Christ!' sung out on an ascending scale, and the congregational response, 'Thanks be to God', echoing it. Smaller candles are lit from the one great light as all stand around the paschal candle and Christ's resurrection is proclaimed in word and song, in the ancient Easter song of praise, the Exultet. Those to be baptized may be initiated at this point, and all renew their baptismal vows around the font. Then follows, either immediately, or later in the morning, the liturgy of the Eucharist, with its high note of joy and praise, in churches adorned with greenery and flowers, with much music and singing, and often dancing and playing of drums and percussion. Many churches celebrate with Easter breakfasts or picnics, or egg hunts and processions.

Yet, dramatic and powerful as the Easter liturgy can be, many women have felt the need to make their own liturgies and to mark the season in their own, particular, ways. As one commentary puts it,

The prescribed liturgies of the Christian churches rarely give scope to women who want to tell the story of God in their lives, and in particular to do so at the most significant time of the Christian year – the days leading up to and including Easter. Many of us have found the traditional Easter liturgies in both content and presentation arid, excluding and seemingly irrelevant to our everyday experiences of death and life.

Interestingly, in vivid contrast to the amount of critical discussion by feminist theologians of the death of Jesus and theologies of salvation and atonement, Eastertide and resurrection have occasioned far less comment or critique. The work of feminist scholars in addressing Easter has been focused largely on retrieving and celebrating the significant role of the women disciples in the gospel resurrection narratives, particularly Mary Magdalene, and reasserting the women's witness and authority. As noted in Chapter 1, there has been some limited, though nevertheless creative and helpful, discussion of what a feminist theology of resurrection might look like. There are some examples of creative feminist liturgies for Easter that celebrate life in all its fullness and women's roles as witnesses, teachers, preachers and leaders in the Church from the earliest days.

This is crucial work, work that requires to be developed and expanded. For, while some seem to assume that Eastertide and resurrection are unproblematic for women, I would suggest precisely the opposite. Beyond the usual questions around the historical basis of belief in the resurrection – what really happened? was the resurrection a 'real' event in real time and space or a symbolic representation of some kind of spiritual transformation? and so on – are other, more pressing questions for women about what it means to claim resurrection here and now in our own lives. Joanna Collicutt McGrath has written recently about the particular challenges to women of being raised with Christ – or, as she puts it, the challenge to 'get up and grow up!'. 'Being raised with Christ is about becoming fully human, reaching our God-given potential, and therefore becoming truly adult,' she suggests, and this process 'involves a move from passive to active, from relaxed to alert, from weak to strong, from sick to well, from dead to alive, from "the world below" to "the world above" (John 8.23), and – perhaps most of all – from lowly to exalted status'. As I have already suggested, the absence of images of a risen Christa points up the need to ask critical questions about why it is that women have not realized narratives or images of their own vitality, empowerment and authority. Why is it that many women are afraid of claiming their own risen status as daughters of God and sisters of Christ? What is it that keeps us clinging to our graves and reluctant to roll away the stone? Women, and men, need active encouragement to continue reading the Christian narrative beyond the chapter that ends with death, bereavement and unspeakable grief. This is not where the Christian narrative ends, and it is not where the journey for the feminine divine ends.

At Noddfa, we made no attempt to mirror or copy the traditional Easter liturgy in all its scope or shape, although we did use many of the same elements. We made our own journey from darkness into morning light, using symbols of fire and candles; we shared symbolic and more substantial food; we read and reinterpreted scriptural stories; we acclaimed the risen Christa in our midst and celebrated in a number of ways. Rising early, while it was still dark, we processed back up the hill where we had left the branches of the cross, carrying firewood and provisions for later. Arriving at the cave, we listened to words inviting us to 'roll back the stone' from our own graves. A fire was eventually lit outside the cave, while violin music was played. Candles were lit from the fire for each woman. Someone proclaimed, 'Jesus died as a Palestinian, Jewish man. Christ rises to be God with us in many different forms – including the Christa.' Then, around the circle, each woman greeted her neighbour with the words, 'Alleluia! We greet the risen Christa in you,' speaking her particular name ('Alleluia! Pat, we greet the risen Christa in you', 'Rosie', 'Chris', 'Helen' and so on), with the person responding 'Alleluia!' Luke's account of Jesus' resurrection was read from John Henson's strikingly fresh version, *Good as New*, in which Jesus greets his friends: 'Hello, good to see you!' We sang a repeated refrain 'Alleluia! alleluia! alleluia!' as light started to spread across the sky and decorated the branches of the tree we had carried up the hill on Friday with coloured ribbons. We took the light and the conviction of risenness into our own bodies through some simple Chi Gon movements, led for us by one of our group. We decorated ourselves with coloured ribbons and created a large coloured decagon, holding it up to the sky and waving it like some giant flag or kite. We greeted each other with words of peace and hugged each other – both to share the joy of the day and to keep warm! We shared tiny golden eggs and hot drinks from flasks, fed the fire, sang songs and enjoyed the space of the new day. Eventually, when we had run out of things to sing, we made our way back down the hill for an enormous breakfast and, later, an even bigger dinner, followed by an egg hunt in the garden and a party that stretched into the evening.

Next day, Easter Monday, we had a playful and creative session in which we explored the idea of what a risen Christa might look like and mean for us, with space for each woman to write, draw, reflect, pray, and then to come together and share our reflections. There was a tremendous outpouring of creativity in this session, and several women wrote powerful poems and reflections on the Christa, while others drew and painted images of a female Christ figure. One woman lay down on the floor and others drew an outline around her body, which was then painted in bold colours and nightlights placed around the outline of the female form. This huge outline of a female form, which took up most of the floor space in the main room where we were eating and meeting, became a focus for shared prayer during the rest of our time together that day and evening.

Easter, of course, is not simply one day in the Christian calendar but a period of fifty days during which the Church celebrates the risen life into which Christ has entered and into which all who walk with Christa are invited to participate. It is a season in which we are invited to live into the reality of our own risen life, something which the calendar recognizes we need time and space to grasp and internalize. Just as the early disciples could not at first comprehend the reality of Christ's resurrection and needed to meet with the risen one in a number of different manifestations and situations, so we too require space and time to grasp what it might mean to be called to be an Easter people and what it can mean to live a risen life – perhaps particularly as women, as those who have been reluctant to let go of our suffering and pain, those who have felt comfortable and safe in clinging to a victim status, those who may be fearful of claiming our own power and capacity for voice and gift and life. Searching for the Christa who is risen and who calls her sisters and friends to enter into that risen space with her is a necessary counterbalance to the recognition of a suffering, crucified Christa, and is the destination towards which this book has been travelling.

At the same time, it is important not to create a false dichotomy between the crucified and the risen Christa, to drive a wedge between them. For the risen one is the crucified one, with the nail prints in her hands, and the crucified one is the risen one, who was not left in abjection but raised into new and glorious life. In the search for a risen Christa who invites women into their own power and risenness, I do not want to valorize a false feminine spirituality which is in denial of the reality of pain, oppression or suffering in women's lives, or appear to be suggesting that it is not possible to know the risen Christa in contexts of suffering, struggle or death. A Christian symbolic, however radically renewed and recreated, will be marked by its commitment to the whole Christ narrative, the story of Jesus which includes both death and resurrection, however we interpret them.

Litany of the women in search of a risen Christa

We seek a religion of natality
not necrophilia

We search for a way of flourishing
rather than decay

We look for a spirituality of birthing
instead of dying

We believe in redemption through peaceful protest
rather than violence

We are the women in search of a risen Christa

We have heard about the man who betrayed you
Speak to us of the woman who anointed you

We know about the man who denied you
Tell us of the woman who spoke up for you

We have heard of the man who carried your cross
Speak to us of the women who wept for you

We know about the men who deserted you
Speak to us of the women who stood by you

We are the women in search of a risen Christa

We have had enough of the symbols of death
Give us the imagery of life

We are sick of sermons on sin
Speak to us the hermeneutics of hope

We have been burdened enough with the weight of guilt
Release in us the energy of possibility

We have been taught too long to emulate weakness
Grow in us our capacity for power

We are the women in search of a risen Christa

Christa, at the door

This is a door that has been closed
for longer than any one woman can remember.

It's the knobless door,
the door going nowhere.

The door in the wall in the garden
outside the city where no one comes.

I'm standing there knocking and pushing and shoving
and scrabbling around for the key

but there's no way in
no way through from this side

After this, I looked: a door stood open.
You were standing there, I couldn't believe it was you.

Look, I have set before you an open door
which no one is able to shut.

Christa, leaving

We never knew that she tried to come back –
not just once, but many times,
in those early weeks when we thought she'd gone for good.
We were absorbed in conversation,
arguing about what to do next,
where we were going to go,
and whether it was safe to be seen together.
We ate a lot and talked, because that was all there was to do.
Food was smuggled in for us by others.
Nothing fancy: bread, olives, fish, a good supply of local
    wine.
We seemed to be perpetually hungry.

Where did she go that first night, and the others in the weeks
    following?
Did she try other doors in other houses in other streets?
Or did she come back to ours,
night after night, varying the time, the light,
hoping this might be the occasion
on which we'd finally open up?

Perhaps she wandered the streets,
loitering in the doorways of shuttered shops,
stopping for a coffee in some late-night bar,
chatting to strangers who, she couldn't help noticing,
had more than enough time for her –
pulling up a chair, offering her cigarettes,
insisting that she share their bottle of wine,
introducing her round the tables.

All the time we remained in the house,
squashed into the inadequate rooms,
only occasionally sending someone out
to restock the food supplies, check up on the local papers,
see if we could find out which way the wind was blowing
    after the trial,
what line the governor was taking now that he'd quashed
    the riots.

We made rules: no one was to leave the house
without permission from one of the eldest.
No one must answer the door.
On no account should we call attention to ourselves
through excess of noise or the amount of rubbish
accumulating. There should be rotas for
cooking, shopping and getting rid of the refuse.

We barricaded ourselves in, settled down for the long haul.
No exits. No entrance for her to come back through.

We never heard from her again.

Places Christa has left

Boardrooms, highly polished vestibules,
the parochial church council's deliberations
about whether to use real bread or wafers.
The Labour Party's discussions about leadership elections.

Trains, except for the empty ones that travel up the west coast
    of Scotland,
mile on mile of sea. Pubs that have become part of chains
where the food is vacuum-packed and microwaved
and she can't afford the astronomical price of the beer.
(She likes small independent ones
in out of the way city suburbs or country villages
where they play folk music and people talk to her at the bar.)

Windowless rooms. Any place where they lock the doors at
    night.
Supermarkets and shopping centres playing canned Muzak
and offering two for the price of one.
She's had enough of airbrushed spaces:
being hemmed in, the pressure on her body,
finding it difficult to breathe or sing.

She's drawn to motorway service stations and garage
    forecourts,
likes their arid anonymity, whiff of danger, strangely
    exhilarating boredom.
She imagines hopping onto the next passing bike
or sneaking into the back of a lorry,
riding endlessly across borders
into countries whose landscapes she's never imagined,
clutching onto the body of some guy she's never met until
    this moment
not knowing his name or destination
having no idea where she'll get off
what place she'll find to leave from next.

Christa, returning

You think she has left
but she has not. She is resting.

You think she has gone underground
but she has not. She has veiled herself.

You think she is powerless
but she is gathering her power,
drawing it back to herself from where it has been dispersed,
   scattered.

You think she is not speaking
only because you do not hear the language of her silence.

You think she is alone
but she has never been.

You think she has lost all her names and seasons
but there have always been those who have kept her ways.

You think that the pattern is broken
but see, she spins the chaos into waves and whorls
you can't yet decipher. Keep looking.

She has never left, though you couldn't find her:
it is we who are returning.

Christa in the night

She would come in the night
where you are sleeping
and take you in her arms in such a way
that you would not wake
but sigh and sighing
settle down deeper into sleep
with her sleeping there beside you

She would come where you sleep
and in your sleeping weep
and without waking you
wipe the tears from your eyes

She would embrace your anxious body
stressed with its pains and disappointments
and without waking you
massage the tension in your shoulders
and ease the burden you find necessary to bear

She would come in the night
where you cry out in your dreams
like a child in a nightmare
searching for the door out of fear

Without waking you would
feel the warmth of her body on your skin
and the first stirrings of birdsong lapping your ears

Christa of the red dress

after Emmanuel Garibay's Emmaus

Christa of the low-cut red dress
the bare arms
the fine boned, olive features
of the laughing eyes
the open mouth
the long, gesticulating arms

I want to sit with you for a long time
like your companions do
in their ordinary, working clothes
eating and drinking in some corner of a favourite club
where the lights are muted and the colours warm

Everyone is talking at once
throwing back their heads and laughing
yet listening to each other too
eyes and hands eager to connect

It doesn't matter how or why you've returned to us
nor that no one knows who you are

It only matters that we are here, now
caught up together in wild abandon
in this unlikely inn of happiness

The Maori Christa

Maybe I've seen her in Auckland, late at night
in some bar on the Karangahape Road, a little drunk,
her eyes all on fire, singing the songs of her people
to a guitar's thick strum.

Or up at Cape Reinga a way off
crouching down under the tree where the spirits depart.
I think she was writing with her finger in the sand,
something impossible to decipher.

On the lawn at Waitangi in front of the Governor's house
I could swear she was listening intently
to the debates of the elders arguing.
She walked away as the dawn light made long shadows
    of the trees.

I've seen her dancing the poi,
swishing the snow-white balls into the air
in rhythm with her swaying body.
We watched, applauding the performance laid on for the
    tourists.

In shops selling greenstone and paua
in the hotels and cafes of Rotorua
in Te Papa and down long rutted roads in the outskirts of
    Taupo
leading to dusty shacks

I've followed her, but never quite caught her.
In the Church of St Faith's I thought I caught her reflection
in a window but it was only my wishful fancy.

I glimpsed an old woman slouched in a caravan
pitched in front of a steaming pool in the Maori village
but she only stared back at me sullenly.

It's not that I want to talk to her, exactly,
since I could only stammer 'Kia ora' and quickly
blunder into silence.

I'd just like to stand for a while in her presence,
ask her to bless me with her mana,
listen to the sound of her voice
consoling or chastising me.

Christa bathing

She lies in the river so still you could easily miss
    her.
Naked, her brown body wrapped in weeds and
    grasses,
she swishes her hands slowly through the warm
    waters
sending little ripples down the stream.
Fantails and swallows dart in and out of the
    Pohutukawa branches,
settle for an instant on her arms –
hairy like the underside of new furled ferns –
fly off again into the forest canopy.

Her face is marked with the ancient symbols of
    her people's art,
dark lines and swirls on her chin.
The patterns mingle with the shadow of leaves,
play of dark and light on the water.

Closing her eyes against the patterns
sleepily cupping the frothy liquid over her body
she lazes in the river's sandbed
making a groove where her body fits.
She's in no hurry to move.

The greenstone round her neck is dark as ivy,
mottled like the moss-covered boulders of rock
that lie strewn along the river.
Precious as the land itself through which the
    river passes
precious as the forests, the mountains
the birds and insects that crowd round her body
precious as the silvery water itself
that never stills for a moment
never exhausts its giving

She is of the greenstone
She is of the mountain
She is of the water

Christa rising

She lies where she lies and has always lain
Hidden apparent
Naked clothed in glory
Dark and light
Mottled and clear
Silent and singing

Christa, crone

after Gillian Allnutt

Her knees will give her hell.
Her joints will hurt.
Her words will all dry up or fly like geese in formation.
She'll take to singing and silence.
Her god-daughters will bake her favourite cakes.
She'll grow a beard.
She'll learn to be untidy.
She'll wear clothes the colour of the sea
and move in them like waves.
She'll hear the voices of the sirens.
She'll talk more to herself and less to others;
she'll weep and laugh in equal measure.
All the poems she's never had time to read
will gather around her like children.
She'll feast on porridge and caviar.
Every day will be a festival ending in darkness.
She'll sleep sound as a bell. No snoring.
The angels will envy her tears.

Her hands

after Jake Lever's Christ Hands

bent in places
where they should not be

impossibly long
black lined, criss-crossed with creases

deep and dark crevices
open at the heart

burning at broken ends
with burnished gold

touching where no other may
in stillness and fire

Only the wounded

Gregory of Nyssa said that he would recognize his sister in
   heaven by her scars.
And I too will be looking for Grampy,
coming towards me limping on his artificial leg
and calling my name that no one else knows me by.
And Mike and John will still be blind, needing to touch my
   face to be sure.
And Donald will need his chair.
I'll have to stoop down low to talk to him
to see whether his face is showing the signs of a bad night, or
   a good one.
And Rach will be talking about some recipe she's craving
even though long sections of her gut are missing
and she shouldn't be eating all that double cream and butter.
And I'll have my long curving wound from belly button to
   below the bikini line,
all my fillings and a wonky left knee.
Or else how will we know ourselves?

We'll be there alongside the company of the famous wounded:
that one-breasted Amazon, Audre, unashamed of her
   asymmetrical torso.
And Virginia, the stones in her pockets and her hair still wet.
Vincent, one side of his face still bandaged up,
and Beethoven, only hearing the internal music.
And Paul, whose thorn in his flesh will finally be revealed for
   what it is.
And Augustine will not be entirely cured of his body's cravings.
And Hildegard will still suffer, on occasion, from migraines.

Christa will wander among us, pouring out Pimms and
   Tequilas,
stopping to place the large glass jugs down from time to time
wincing where it still hurts her to lift,
the scars in her wrist white where they'll never heal over
   completely
and her silver-thonged sandals unable to disguise the red
   marks on her feet.

128

The only ones who won't be there are the prematurely perfect
whose bodies have had all sickness manicured out of them
whose every desire has been more than amply satisfied
who have no need of heaven
having vacated the earth of their pain.

The markings of the body
are not always obvious like
tattoos, piercings, scars on visible parts,
hair outrageously coloured or dyed.

Invisible to the naked eye,
they ache at night
when roused from sleep for no apparent reason.

They smart when the body is touched
in desire, need or rejection
or blurt their pain in the middle of parties, classes, bus
    journeys.

You may seek to hide them or present them for healing
to any number of competent doctors, therapists, surgeons.
They will not be effaced or eroded.

Enduring as faint scratches, fissures, blotches, lumps or
    imbalances,
they are the body's gestures towards its own resurrection,
fragile tissues of wounded transcendence.

Shekinah

after Melissa Raphael

Wherever there is a bending over
a protective covering of vulnerable flesh

Wherever one person strokes
with the intention to warm, reassure, heal

Wherever there is a gesture
towards feeding, cleaning

(no matter that the bin is empty,
water too precious or filthy for washing)

Wherever there is a lifting up
from the mud and the gutter

and a holding of lice-infected mortality
close to the heart and the lungs

Wherever one weakened hand
reaches across intolerable pain or loss

to touch another who does not
speak the same language

Wherever the imperative of care
endures despite any difference it can make

Wherever the bearing is borne
in the bodies of those

who should, themselves, by right
long since have expired

there, there –
                She is resurrected there

A risen woman

Easter Monday, Noddfa

A risen woman does not fear death.
She has been to the grave and come back again.
She knows she may return there.

A risen woman bears in her body
the marks of her many dyings and risings,
though not all her scars may be seen.

A risen woman appears to her friends as strange and yet
    familiar,
as transformed and as she has always been.
Sometimes they will recognize her. Often they will not.

A risen woman never rises alone.
She brings with her all whom she loves and many she does
    not know.
They are borne in her rising.

A risen woman touches all she meets with healing and hope.
In her eyes we see the glimpse of our own rising.

A risen woman will not give easy assurances.
She does not lie about the cost of rising.

Look at her! Though the forces of death that tried to pull her
    back were legion,
her resistance is awesome. She flings herself full tilt into living.

A risen woman does not find enough risen sisters to join her.
Too many are still clinging to their graves.
She is calling out to them, saying:

'Do not be afraid! Have courage!
Come out! Uncover your faces!'

A risen woman has compassion for the ones who can't follow
    her yet,
though her heart is breaking for so much life denied.

A risen woman knows the taste of her own tears
as she moves into the solitude of freedom.

7

The kin-dom of Christa

Ascension and after

Ascensiontide is an embarrassment to the Christian who reads the New Testament in any kind of literalist sense. With its hierarchical spatial topography and all those ridiculous paintings of the disciples crowded round gazing up into the sky at Jesus' disappearing feet, it only seems bizarre or comical to the positivist mind. But theologically and existentially, Ascensiontide is absolutely essential to the Christian narrative, and utterly serious, not least in its import for contemporary feminists – though I realize as I write this that I can't think of a single feminist reflection on the Ascension, suggesting that feminists, too, find it something of an embarrassment or an irrelevance.

Nevertheless, the Ascension is central to the Christian narrative, and not some mere addendum, because it is about the leave-taking of Christ, the necessary departure of God. Even the risen one – the one who has been revealed as the ongoing presence of God whom violence and death cannot defeat – must rise again, out of our lives' earthly orbit, out of any kind of grasp or knowledge we have acquired of him/her, out of our hands and our future. There is a certain brutality at this point of the Christian narrative, although it is not played up in the New Testament. For it is another kind of death, following fast on the heels of the cross and the loss of Christ in that bloody death. No sooner is the Christ restored to his friends and disciples, they just begin to get their heads and their hearts around his new, strange, unpredictable, uncontainable risen presence, and he is off again – this time for good. No more touching him, being touched by him, speaking to him, eating with him, feasting their eyes upon him. No more questions answered, explanations, directives, instructions. It is necessary for the Christ to ascend, they are told, so that the Spirit can be given. They have to risk losing the one who has been restored to them all over again.

133

The paradigm for this radical loss is Mary Magdalene's encounter with the risen Christ in the garden, something I wrote about some twenty years ago in my first solo book, *Easter Garden*:

The command to go, to leave her beloved whom she has now so newly found, was perhaps experienced by Mary as a harsh and bitter blow, a rejection and denial of the intimacy she longs to prolong ... Yet, as she obeys the Lord's command – unwillingly, fearfully, even begrudgingly – she discovers the deeper miracle and truth of the resurrection, which, until now, she could not know. She finds that Christ is there, wherever she goes, the living one present with her, within her, beside her and before her, not simply manifest in the particular space and time of the garden encounter, but released in the world everywhere. As she goes out to proclaim the message of his resurrection, Christ himself has gone before her and comes after her. He makes himself present again in the company of his disciples and friends, and teaches them that henceforth he will be with them always in the power and presence of the Spirit. He is no longer to be known within the confines of his own physical body, but will manifest himself in the body of his believers, in the bodies of those who love him and receive him, in the lovely body of the earth itself. Earth, air, sky, sun, moon, water, fire and all that is within the world henceforth have become God's body and proclaim God's glory.

And Mary, too, must learn to know him [*sic*] in this bigger, wider, deeper, freer way. She who had defined herself wholly in terms of her relationship to him, her saviour, healer, lover, lord and friend, is now to let him go, and find herself and her God in a new freedom and openness of being. Released from the bonds of a clinging, cloying love and dependency upon Jesus, she is to become her own true self in freedom and share that self freely and generously with other selves – friends, lovers, sisters, brothers. She who had first met and known God in the beloved body of Jesus is now to meet and know the same divine presence in her own beloved woman's body, in the body of other believers, in the body of all God's creatures, in the body of the world. Paradoxically, only by thus stepping out into separation and freedom, by letting her Christ go freely, will she find him and know him in all the abundance of wholeness, joy and fullness which he promises. Unfettered by time and space, unlimited by the physical body which Mary had loved and has learned to let go, the Lord will be with them and among them in radically new and unexpected ways.

One of these 'new and unexpected ways' may, of course, be the Christa, bursting the bounds of the patriarchal representations of God which, even in that earlier book, I could not entirely break free of (and if I would change anything now in the passage above, it would be the masculine gender to speak of Christ). Yet the paradox continues: even the Christa, the female form of the risen Christ, so newly realized and grasped by artists and theologians in our own time, only just coming into her own fullness, has to depart. She is no final resting place for the Christological journey, no final feminist word about God, no absolute icon of divinity. Like every helpful, creative symbol or story of the divine, she is incomplete, she is provisional. She must be cherished and assimilated but then released, let go of, lost to her own larger reality, to her own future momentum.

Only so can the Spirit come and be released into the community of those who love God. Christa has to depart so that the kin-dom of Christa may flourish, so that women and men may learn to look to one another, and to the non-human creatures of the earth, as those who now incarnate the body of Christa. These are the ones who now demand our full attention, love and cherishing. Rather than gazing up into the heavens where Christa departs, we are to embrace the body of God in our own temporal locations and occupations, finding her wherever we turn and travel and touch.

So, although Christa does appear in some of the pieces that follow, the focus isn't so much on her as on the community of her sisters, brothers, friends and family members who are, now, her ongoing presence in the world; and on the ongoing dynamic of finding and losing, arriving and departing, affirmation and negation that has been present throughout this book, and from which there is no final escape. Christa must be lost, loosed, let loose – to rise, ascend, disperse, and be refound in all kinds of new people, places and ways, including some rather unlikely ones. Only so can the Spirit of Christa be released in a fuller, larger, freer way. And so this chapter celebrates, in some quite literal as well as metaphorical ways, the notion of large and loose women as those in whom the Spirit of Christa is now to be found. This is, at one and the same time, to challenge some of the stereotypes of femininity which dictate that women should be small, petite, neat, confined and contained, not take up too much room in the world, and to insist that the Spirit of Christa is a spirit of freedom, largesse and amplitude, unable to be confined within any of the narrow spaces religion, culture or church might seek to contain her. Where the Spirit of Christa abounds, all constraints and narrowness will be subverted, and the kin-dom of Christa celebrated as a place of enormous, indeed limitless, proportions – the 'wide space' the psalmist speaks of as the place into which God brings all who respond to the divine call.

Christa on the loose

such a fast one

you came running towards us
over the morning grass

then off, off forth on swing
sweeping smooth on a big wind
out of our sight

I want to come with you
fly with you

away   away
all my life   longing to soar   catch fire
as kingfishers do

'where I am going you cannot come'

you have rebuffed me
taking yourself away   away

teaching my heart to break   gash   blue-bleak
leap out of its bony cage
soar   scatter after you   into sunlight

The family of Christa

She stopped counting a long time ago:
sisters, half-sisters, step-brothers,
adoptive aunts, cousins, second cousins once removed,
great-grandparents by marriage,
ancestors by clan and distant kinship,
or just because they met once and knew they'd be
    kin for ever.
In the end, safer to call everyone
sister, brother, mother, father,
without qualification or explanation.

There's always room for another at the table, anyhow.
Shift along, budge up, lay an extra place,
squeeze another chair in.
Always cook some extra, she tells her children.
Expect the unexpected:
the girlfriend sleeping over
the relatives who just happened to be passing.
And when, rarely, she sits to eat alone,
the room is full of presences:
her solitary table sighs with the weight
of all those lives that have sat around it.
She relishes the taste
from the bowl that has been clasped
and passed around the circle
by so many loved, forgotten, remembered hands.

It doesn't matter that she can't recall names.
Faces she never forgets,
voices will conjure up their pasts,
and everyone she's ever met
jostles somewhere thickly in her body
each one connected to the other
though more than half of them would be startled to discover
they are family, after all.

Love is what happens
Vaughan Park, May–July 2009

when you arrive in a place alone
a long way from home
set your bags down
breathe in the air of the sea
slip into the pattern of a place
get on with what it is you came to do
(read, write, pray, walk the beach)

because you didn't need to defend your heart against anything
because you were met with kindness and warmth
because there was a spacious welcome here in host and house
because you were given all the time in the world you needed
because the place held you like an empty cup in its hands
and the days and the nights filled it to overflowing

because of light falling on water
and the sound of waves at night falling on sleep
because of the cadences of voices you came to love
rising and falling in quiet rhythm in the chapel
because of starlight and candlelight and moonlight

and look, it is time to leave
and the holy gathers into a crescendo of touching and holding
    and wounding
and these days will never be given again
and these days will be with me for ever

and the love I was born for has happened again
in a place full of strangers
who took me in and brought me home
and sent me on my way again

never the same always the same woman
healed   held   hurting
                        homeward bound

Loose women

Loose women never stay long in one place
are not to be trusted when they look in your eyes
tell you they'll be back soon

Loose women are profligate with their affections as with their
    purses
give their hearts and their silver to any old boozer

Loose women lose addresses and friends easily
find new ones
move on to the next bar
next open door   open heart

Loose women scatter words and songs about
make declarations of love, promises
stories that are never the same twice in the telling

Loose women are reckless with their loves as their lives
not caring whose bed they shack up in for a night
generous with their soft ample bodies

Loose women cannot be contained
by those who want to fix them
will never settle down

Loose women are free as clouds
as the wind   as water
as Christa   risen   on her way
                    disappeared

Fat Christa

for Lisa Isherwood

In praise of her amplitude
her huge breasts that suckle children
resting on the belly rolls she's given up trying to hide
her arms and legs sturdy as tree trunks
that have stood in the forest for centuries

In praise of her enormous body
wide as a world
diffused in the dimpled flesh of the earth
folds and ripples of rolling fields
mounds that are hillocks, tors and mountains (her breasts)
cavernous underground caves (her womb)
and dark running waters (her blood)
the heaving heat of her constantly beating heart

A canticle in praise of large women

Maya Angelou, I salute you:
more regal than the queen,
you walked into the marquee at Hay
and two thousand people rose to applaud you,
but might just as well have fallen to their knees.

Hail, Lisa Isherwood! Hoorah for your fat theology
and your own solid, indefatigable frame
that isn't going to shift out of the way of heteropatriarchy.
You clear a space for desires as large as we can make them,
teach us to name our hungers big,
give us a fleshy Christ of womanly abundance,
and a God bigger than any we've imagined.

Blessings on you, June Boyce-Tillman,
woman of unstoppable energy and creativity:
out of your loose largesse have tumbled
songs to inspire and include,
words that dance and embrace,
operas and choir works to fill our cathedrals.

Helen Cameron, friend, sister and colleague:
your appetite for life is insatiable.
You work and live more hours than you or any woman
    should
and sometimes I could shake you for it,
but I love you with your loud laugh and extravagant shoes.
You've devoured more novels and plays than any person
    I know
and out of that unbounded store
you feed those who are hungry for the unmarked ways of
    God.

You women who are unafraid to know your appetites and
    indulge them,
who take up all the space you want without apology,
who pluck the fruit from the tree and eat it down to the
    last pip
then reach out your hands to take another, and another . . .

142

You have brought God out of the airy heavens and down
  to earth,
growing divinity in the flesh of the world,
making her big, bigger, bursting all bounds.

Praise be to you, source of all life and lusciousness,
scent, savour and taste, yearning and grasping,
questing and sighing.
Teach us to reach for the fruit of the tree of knowledge
and not to feel guilty.

Christa, listening

She listens with her whole body
to what others never even realize
is there to be heard.

Out of the ground she calls forth
the prayer of the earth.

She hears a singer's song before the singer knows it.
For days it trembles on her lips like electricity;
at last the singer opens his mouth
and knows his own song.

She listens where others never bother
to the mute child
to the so-called dumb animals.

She wakes early to the dawn chorus
of road sweepers and office cleaners
up long ahead of the city commuters.
She is familiar with the warm boozy strains of jazz
from the nightclubs at 3 a.m.
and the love-cries of teenagers making out in cars
in tucked-away city roads.

She knows the hour and the half-hour
at which the babies wake around the globe
and dazed parents rouse themselves for the night feed.
She knows the grateful sound of the light clicking off
and the soft snores of bodies that fall back, instantly, to sleep.

She hears the voices that never speak in the councils of
    the wise
and the wisdom of their silence.
She hears the suffering of those that never complain
though their sorrows cry out to heaven.
She knows the bone-weariness of the incessant talker
and the fear of the ones who can't keep silent.
She detects the cynicism of the prattlers who've
talked themselves out of whatever idealism they once knew.

Out of her listening she is readying herself to speak,
if only anyone can be found ready to listen.

Oblation

Malling Abbey

Coming here in season and out,
over years; to feel the cold at sundown
enter my bones, separate out
wanting and the desire of the heart.
To sleep the sleep of the righteous
in the narrow bed where archbishops have slept,
and abbots and professors,
in the high beamed room up the creaking stairs
over the pilgrim chapel. To wake
into dark, dress against the chill,
hurry to the concrete church
where the sisters shuffle in – aged and bent, many of them,
    now
but their voices are the virginal notes of girls
rising and emptying into the enormous space above
    our heads.
Consider the offering
of their lives, and mine, on the altar.
Fearing death and decline, wanting to give myself.
Drawing back. All that is not yet
gathered. Knowing I shall go and come again,
innumerable times, in the years that remain.
Gathering what is scattered,
seeding what has been gathered.
Listen to the burbling stream falling over stones,
count fallen leaves banked up in water.

Becoming divine

after Grace Jantzen

Eliciting our voices
in the speech of our mothers and daughters

Listening to the lacunae
the sounds from the margins

Practising our difference
exploiting it, expanding it

Pushing up against the horizon of divinity
discovering there our own subjectivity

Re-possessing what has been taken from us
the feminine imaginary

Re-conceiving ourselves as god, goddess
the field of creativity, fertility, fecundity

Opening up the domain of the new
the symbolic future, a mode of transcendence

Moving into the divine erotic
the cascade and avalanche of freedom

Christa ascending

Having found her so late
how should I lose her so soon?

Having grasped the flesh of her
– solid, breathing, sweet smelling –

how should my hands fall empty
out of the singing air?

Having eaten daily of her bread
must I now practise
the Eucharist of absence?

Having sought her down the nights and days
dreamed her   held her fast
must she now be lost to me for ever?

Running after her, panting
I only caught a glimpse of her dark heels
a swathe of hair
as she disappeared into the night forest

All that is left to me now
is a faint trace of her perfume

a memory of the air
dancing   parting   swaying

where now she is
                                  gone

Christa collects

for Stephen

Advent and Christmas

Christa, God's beloved,
born incognito in our midst,
strange to us yet common as any baby:
teach us to recognize you,
to cherish you, care for you, and honour you
in your endless becoming among us.

Christa, born among us as the poorest black baby,
surviving disease, malnutrition, illiteracy,
war, flood and drought,
enduring the world's repeated indignities:
come, show us your power,
overturn the structures of injustice that murder and maim,
render all our idolatries void.

Christa, lying helpless on your mother's lap,
looking to a human breast for nourishment
and a human home for protection:
may we be so moved by your naked helplessness
that we learn to show compassion
to all the world's children.

Christa, our sister,
come to us in female flesh,
tasting the danger and delight of any young
    girl's growing;
bleeding as we bleed,
loving as we love,
learning to claim our womanly power
as God's redemptive presence in the world.

Maundy Thursday

Christa our healer,
shifter of the hot spring pools,
mover of the rising steam:
massage our aching limbs with your heat
rub the dark mineral muds into our flesh
relax our bodies in your watery arms
until every last inch of resistance is taken from us
and we sleep the undreaming sleep of the
    surrendered.

Christa our sister,
come spread your table in our midst.
Break the bread of freedom with us.
Pour the wine of your jouissance over us.
Call us to feast with you,
dance with you and delight with you
where you banquet among us
at the tables of the poor.

Good Friday

Christa, God's chosen yet rejected by men;
daily beaten, raped and crucified
wherever female flesh is abhorred and abused:
reveal to us your broken form in the suffering of
    our sisters
that we may bear you up, bind and tend your body,
staunch the wounds
that will otherwise bleed to eternity.

We adore you, Christa the kenosis of patriarchy,
pouring out your privilege
divesting yourself of all assumed status
disarming the powers that would bind.
Embolden us to challenge every system that constrains
    you
every hierarchy that robs our sisters and brothers
    of life.

Eastertide

Christa, God's risen,
dazzling in your beauty,
radiant in your power:
stand among us,
breathe on us,
touch us in our wounded places,
that we may share in your risen glory
and so become good news to a suffering world.

Ascensiontide

Christa, ascending one,
leaving as suddenly as you have come to us:
teach us not to cling to you,
even as we smart with the pain of your departure,
but to let you go where you will
so that we may claim our own power in the world.

Spirit of Christa,
kindle the flame of your presence among us,
descend upon us and empower us to know who we are:
icons of your christic community,
God's beloved in the world.

Notes, sources and acknowledgements

Preface

Page x. The text of my Good Friday addresses at St James, Piccadilly, can be found on the St James website at <http://www.st-james-piccadilly.org/sermon-texts.html> (under Good Friday 2 April 2010).

1 Seeking the risen Christa

1 Joanna Collicutt McGrath has recently written of the tendency among many women to imagine Jesus as a romantic hero figure, rather in the manner of a Mr Darcy, upon whom their projected needs, hopes and expectations can be focused. While Collicutt McGrath suggests that this tendency to seek out hero figures may not necessarily be unhealthy and may meet profound psychological needs, at least for a time, there is the danger of 'get[ting] stuck in certain patterns of relating to Jesus that can make it difficult to get up and move on'. See Joanna Collicutt McGrath, *Jesus and the Gospel Women* (London: SPCK, 2009), p. 1 and ch. 1 generally.

2 See Elisabeth Moltmann-Wendel, *The Women Around Jesus* (London: SCM Press, 1982), ch. 3.

3 My first book, *Easter Garden: A Sequence of Readings on the Easter Hope* (London: Fount, 1990), charts something of this journey out of the Edenic garden of childhood into the open space of womanhood.

4 For an overview and review, see my *Faith and Feminism: An Introduction to Christian Feminist Theology* (London: Darton, Longman and Todd, 2003), ch. 5.

5 See Mary Daly, *Beyond God the Father: Towards a Philosophy of Women's Liberation*, 2nd edn (London: Women's Press, 1986); Naomi Goldenberg, *Changing of the Gods: Feminism and the End of Traditional Religions* (Boston: Beacon Press, 1979); Daphne Hampson, *Theology and Feminism* (Oxford: Blackwell, 1990).

6 Karen Trimble Alliaume, quoted in Mary McClintock Fulkerson, *Changing the Subject: Women's Discourses and Feminist Theology* (Minneapolis, MN: Fortress Press, 1994), p. x.

7 See <www.edwinasandys.com>. The image is also included in the study pack, *The Christ We Share*, 2nd edn (London: USPG, 2000).

8 At <www.dittwald.com/torontosculpture>.

9 Julie Clague, 'The Christa: Symbolizing My Humanity and My Pain', *Feminist Theology* 14.1 (2005), pp. 83–108.

10 Kittredge Cherry, *Art That Dares: Gay Jesus, Woman Christ, and More* (Berkeley, CA: AndroGyne Press, 2007). See also her website, <www.jesusinlove.org>, especially 'Alternative images of Christ and Mary' under 'Links'.

11 See Cherry, *Art That Dares*, <www.jesusinlove.org> for examples of these works.

12 For example, Renée Cox's *Yo Mama's Last Supper*, a 5-panel colour portrayal with Cox herself as a naked Christ figure surrounded by twelve black apostles – at <http://www.geektimes.com/michael/site/archive/2001/03-01/images/ReneeCoxYoMamasLastSupper.jpg> – and François Girbauld's portrayal of the Last Supper with female Christ and eleven female disciples, one male, at <http://adsoftheworld.com/media/print/marithe_francois_girbaud_last_supper>.

13 For example, a whole sequence of stylized photographs of a female crucified Christ can be found on the Passion of a Goddess site, at <http://www.passionofagoddess.com>.

14 See <http://femalechristinarts.com>, Movies, for examples of video versions of the Christa. Warning: some of these may be considered pornographic in content and approach.

15 Rosemary Radford Ruether, *Sexism and God-Talk* (London: SCM Press, 1983), p. 138.

16 Carter Heyward, *Speaking of Christ: A Lesbian Feminist Voice* (New York: Pilgrim Press, 1989), p. 21.

17 Heyward, *Speaking of Christ*, p. 22.

18 Heyward, *Speaking of Christ*, p. 84.

19 Daly, *Beyond God the Father*, pp. 74–5.

20 Audre Lorde, 'Uses of the Erotic: The Erotic as Power', in *The Audre Lorde Compendium* (London: Pandora, 1996), pp. 106–12.

21 Susan Griffin, *Pornography and Silence: Culture's Revenge Against Nature* (New York: Harper & Row, 1981), *Woman and Nature: The Roaring Inside Her* (New York: Harper & Row, 1979).

22 Adrienne Rich, *A Wild Patience Has Taken Me This Far: Poems 1978–1981* (New York: W. W. Norton, 1981).

23 Rita Nakashima Brock, *Journeys by Heart: A Christology of Erotic Power*, 2nd edn (Eugene, OR: Wipf & Stock, 2008), p. 113.

24 Brock, *Journeys by Heart*, p. 52.

25 Brock, *Journeys by Heart*, p. 97.

26 Brock, *Journeys by Heart*, pp. 103–4.

27 For instance, James Cone and J. Deotis Roberts developed the notion of a black Christ in core texts such as Cone's *A Black Theology of Liberation* (New York: Lippincott, 1970) and Roberts' *A Black Political Theology* (Philadelphia: Westminster Press, 1974) – a concept which leaders of the

black struggle such as Martin Luther King and Malcolm X had previously articulated. See Kelly Brown Douglas, *The Black Christ* (Maryknoll, NY: Orbis Books, 1994) for a review and discussion of the development of the notion of the black Christ in the work of black and womanist theologians.

28 The text of the speech can be found in a number of different forms, including at wikipedia.org.

29 Jacquelyn Grant, 'Womanist Theology: Black Women's Experience as a Source for Doing Theology, with Special Reference to Christology', *Journal of the Interdenominational Theological Center* 13.2 (1986), pp. 195–212.

30 Douglas, *The Black Christ*, p. 108.

31 Douglas, *The Black Christ*, p. 177.

32 Quoted by Donald Eadie, 'More than Eucharistic Liturgies and Eucharistic Living', in Stephen Burns, Nicola Slee and Michael N. Jagessar (eds), *The Edge of God: New Liturgical Texts and Contexts in Conversation* (London: Epworth, 2008), p. 15.

33 See, for example, Stephen Burns, '"Four in a Vestment?" Feminist Gestures for Christian Assembly', Anita Monro, '"And Ain't I a Woman": The Phonetic Dramaturgy of Feeding the Family', and Alastair Barrett, '*In persona Christae*: Towards a Feminist Political Christ-( )-logy of Presiding; or, How Presiding with Children Trains Us to Challenge "the Powers that Be"', in Nicola Slee and Stephen Burns (eds), *Presiding Like a Woman* (London: SPCK, 2010), pp. 9–18, 123–32, 166–77.

34 Chung Hyun Kyung, *Struggle to Be the Sun Again: Introducing Asian Women's Theology* (London: SCM Press, 1991), ch. 4.

35 Kwok Pui-lan, 'God Weeps with Our Pain', and Lee Oo Chung, 'One Woman's Confession of Faith', in John S. Pobee and Bärbel von Wartenberg-Potter (eds), *New Eyes for Reading: Biblical and Theological Reflections by Women from the Third World* (Geneva: WCC, 1986), pp. 90–5 and pp. 18–20; Marianne Katoppo, 'Mother Jesus', in Alison O'Grady (ed.), *Voices of Women: An Asian Anthology* (Singapore: Asian Christian Women's Conference, 1978).

36 Park Soon Kyung, *The Korean Nation and the Task of Women's Theology* (Seoul: Daehan Keedokyo Suhwe, 1983), p. 51.

37 Choi Man Ja, 'Feminist Christology', Consultation on Asian Women's Theology, Singapore, November 1987, *In God's Image* (December 1987), p. 8.

38 Virginia Fabella, 'Asian Women and Christology', *In God's Image* (September 1987), pp. 15.

39 Marcella Althaus-Reid, *Indecent Theology: Theological Perversions in Sex, Gender and Politics* (London: Routledge, 2000), p. 111.

40 Althaus-Reid, *Indecent Theology*, p. 116.

41 Althaus-Reid, *Indecent Theology*, p. 111.

42 Althaus-Reid, *Indecent Theology*, p. 111.

43 Lisa Isherwood, *The Fat Jesus: Feminist Explorations in Boundaries and Transgressions* (London: Darton, Longman and Todd, 2007).

44 Isherwood, *The Fat Jesus*, p. 114.

45 Isherwood, *The Fat Jesus*, pp. 7, 118–19.

46 Isherwood, *The Fat Jesus*, p. 142.

47 In Clague, 'The Christa', p. 86.

48 Sheila Redmond, '"Remember the good, forget the bad": Denial and family violence in a Christian worship service', in Marjorie Procter-Smith and Janet R. Walton (eds), *Women at Worship: Interpretations of North American Diversity* (Louisville, KY: Westminster/John Knox Press, 1993), p. 78.

49 I have not been able to trace the original source of this poem.

50 Edwina Hunter, quoted in Clague, 'The Christa', p. 87.

51 Ivone Gebara, *Out of the Depths: Women's Experience of Evil and Salvation* (Minneapolis, MN: Fortress Press, 2002), p. 117.

52 Ruether, *Sexism and God-Talk*, ch. 5.

53 For example, Tina Beattie argues for the positive value of Jesus' masculinity: 'Christ took on the phallus in order to expose the "big, hard, up" lie which sanctions male power and brutalizes the male body . . . When Christ becomes the sinful male body, he liberates women as well as men from the domination of the phallus.' 'Sexuality and the Resurrection of the Body: Reflections in a Hall of Mirrors', in Gavin D'Costa (ed.), *Resurrection Reconsidered* (Oxford: Oneworld Publications, 1996), p. 142. Similarly, J'annine Jobling has recently argued for the positive significance of the masculinity of Jesus in 'Post-Christian Hermeneutics: The Rise and Fall of Female Subjectivity', in Lisa Isherwood and Kathleen McPhillips (eds), *Post-Christian Feminisms: A Critical Approach* (Aldershot: Ashgate, 2008), pp. 89–104.

54 See my early article, 'Parables and Women's Experience', *The Modern Churchman* 26.2 (1984), pp. 20–31, reproduced in A. Loades (ed.), *Feminist Theology: A Reader* (London: SPCK, 1990), pp. 41–7.

55 See, for example, Dorothy Lee, *Flesh and Glory: Symbolism, Gender and Theology in the Gospel of John* (New York: Crossroad, 2002); Kathleen P. Rushton, 'The (Pro)creative Parables of Labour and Childbirth (John 3.1–10 and 16.21–22)', in Mary Ann Beavis (ed.), *The Lost Coin: Parables of Women, Work, and Wisdom* (Sheffield: Sheffield Academic Press, 2002), pp. 206–29; Amy-Jill Levine with Marianne Blickenstaff (eds), *A Feminist Companion to John*, Vols 1 and 2 (Sheffield: Sheffield Academic Press, 2003). For an excellent summary of recent readings of feminine imagery in John, with full references, see Barbara E. Reid, *Taking Up the Cross: New Testament Interpretations Through Latina and Feminist Eyes* (Minneapolis, MN: Fortress Press, 2007), ch. 5.

56 Reid, *Taking Up the Cross*, p. 167.

57 For a summary of the significance of Wisdom, see 'Sophia/Wisdom', in Letty M. Russell and J. Shannon Clarkson (eds), *Dictionary of Feminist Theologies* (Louisville, KY: Westminster/John Knox Press and London: Mowbray, 1996), pp. 268–70, and Susan Cole, Marian Ronan and Hal Taussig, *Wisdom's Feast: Sophia in Study and Celebration,* new edn (Kansas City: Sheed & Ward, 1996). Wisdom Christologies have been developed by a range of feminists, perhaps most notably Elizabeth Johnson in *She Who Is: The Mystery of God in Feminist Theological Discourse* (New York: Crossroad, 1992), and Elisabeth Schüssler Fiorenza in *Jesus: Miriam's Child, Sophia's Prophet* (London: SCM Press, 1995).

58 This prayer can be found in numerous sources online, for example at <http://www.poetseers.org/spiritual_and_devotional_poets/christian/ teresa_of_avila/prayers_and_works/>. In fact, there is no surviving evidence that Teresa is indeed the source of this famous saying, although she is well established in many anthologies as the source.

59 Julian of Norwich, *Revelations of Divine Love* (Harmondsworth: Penguin, 1966), chs 57 onwards, especially ch. 60 (pp. 169–71).

60 See, for example, images of the wounds of Christ on prayer rolls and prayer sheets in *The Image of Christ: The Catalogue of the Exhibition Seeing Salvation* (London: National Gallery Company Ltd, 2000), ch. 5.

61 For a fascinating account of women's medieval mysticism, see Caroline Walker Bynum, *Jesus as Mother: Studies in the Spirituality of the High Middle Ages* (Los Angeles: University of California Press, 1982), helpfully summarized in Isherwood, *The Fat Jesus*, pp. 52ff.

62 For a good summary of the arguments used by medieval theologians about the gender of Jesus, see Janet Martin Soskice, 'Blood and Defilement: Christology', in *The Kindness of God: Metaphor, Gender, and Religious Language* (Oxford: Oxford University Press, 2008), pp. 84–5.

63 See Ruether, *Sexism and God-Talk*, p. 36.

64 For a brief account of the cult of Wilgefortis, see Wikipedia. For a more scholarly and detailed account, see Ilse E. Friesen, *The Female Crucifix: Images of St Wilgefortis since the Middle Ages* (Waterloo, Ontario: Wilfred Laurier University Press, 2001).

65 And addressing her in my prayers – see, for example, the Eucharistic Prayer in *Praying Like a Woman* (London: SPCK, 2004), pp. 124–5.

66 Garibay has painted a number of versions of this episode, in which a vibrant Filipina female Christ shares wine and bread with a small, intimate group of friends. See <www.asianchristianart.org/galleries/resurrection/pages/ Garibay.html>.

67 *A Tribute to Matthias* by Jill Ansell, *c.*1991, in Cherry, *Art That Dares*, p. 24. Also see her Missa Solemnis at <http://jesusinlove.org/art-that-dares. php#gallery>.

68 In Cherry, *Art That Dares*, pp. 55 and 69.

69 Mary Daly, *Gyn/Ecology: The Metaethics of Radical Feminism* (London: Women's Press, 1978), pp. 59–60, and ch. 2.

70 See particularly Grace Jantzen, *Becoming Divine: Towards a Feminist Philosophy of Religion* (Manchester: Manchester University Press, 1998), ch. 6.

71 Gebara, *Out of the Depths*, p. 118.

72 Gebara, *Out of the Depths*, p. 120.

73 Gebara, *Out of the Depths*, p. 121.

74 Gebara, *Out of the Depths*, p. 122.

75 Gebara, *Out of the Depths*, p. 123.

76 Gebara, *Out of the Depths*, p. 124.

77 Gebara, *Out of the Depths*, p. 125.

78 Althaus-Reid, *Indecent Theology*, p. 123.

79 Sheila Redmond describes Lutkenhause-Lackey's *Crucified Woman* as 'anorexic' in her extreme thinness, inviting the kind of critique of the idolization of the thin female body that Lisa Isherwood has developed in her *Fat Jesus*.

2 Come as a girl

Page 31. The section on Shakespeare's sister can be found in Virginia Woolf, *A Room of One's Own* (London: Granada, 1977), section 3, pp. 46ff.

Page 31. Janet Martin Soskice briefly reviews arguments about whether Christ might have been born female in 'Blood and Defilement: Christology', in her collection *The Kindness of God: Metaphor, Gender, and Religious Language* (Oxford: Oxford University Press, 2008), p. 85. The quotation from Aquinas is from the *Summa Theologiae* 3a, 31, 4 (London: Eyre & Spottiswoode, 1964).

Page 32, 'boys are best'. See Sylvia's letter to God ('Dear God, are boys better than girls? I know you are one but try to be fair'), in Stuart Hample and Eric Marshall (compilers), *Children's Letters to God* (London: Collins, 1967), reprinted several times in the USA and UK.

Page 32. There is little literature on the faith of girls, but see Dori Grinenko Baker, *Doing Girlfriend Theology: God-Talk with Young Women* (Cleveland: Pilgrim Press, 2007); Joyce Ann Mercer, *Girltalk, Godtalk: Why Faith Matters to Teenage Girls – and Their Parents* (San Francisco: Jossey-Bass, 2008). Anne Phillips' study, *The Faith of Girls: Children's Spirituality and Transition into Adulthood* (Aldershot: Ashgate, forthcoming) represents the most significant scholarly study in the UK to date.

Page 34, 'Christa, becoming'. This poem has taken inspiration from a number of sources, and draws on them freely. Comments by Marcella Althaus-Reid on the significance of the girl in her essay 'The Bi/girl Writings: From Feminist Theology to Queer Theologies', in *Post-Christian Feminisms: A Critical Approach* (Aldershot: Ashgate, 2008), pp. 112–13, were particularly suggestive in sparking off the poem. Alice Walker's well-known definition of 'womanist' is quoted liberally at the end of the poem, from *In Search of our Mother's Gardens* (San Diego, CA: Harcourt Brace Jovanovich, 1983), pp. xi–xii. Dori Grinenko Baker explores the significance of Walker's notion of Womanism for girls in *Doing Girlfriend Theology*. Most of all, I am indebted to the doctoral research of Anne Phillips on the faith of adolescent girls, which I have been privileged to supervise. See Anne Phillips, 'Girls in Transition, Self in Relationship in Early Adolescence: A Study of Girls Aged 11–13, Their Faith and Spiritual Growth in Baptist Churches', unpublished PhD thesis, University of Manchester, 2009, and *The Faith of Girls*. Anne has taught me to read certain scriptural stories about girls in new ways, and I draw on her reading of these stories, as well as the texts themselves, in the body of the poem. The scriptural texts referred to are: Jairus' daughter (Mark 5.21–43; Matthew 9.18–26; Luke 8.40–56); Miriam (Exodus 2.1–10); Lo-ruhamah, the only named girl in the Hebrew Scriptures (Hosea 1.6, 8; 2.1); Naaman's wife's slave girl (2 Kings 5.2–3).

Page 37, 'Christa growing up'. Again, it was Anne Phillips who alerted me to the text in Ezekiel on which this poem is based, which speaks of the origins of Jerusalem via the metaphor of a daughter born in a foreign land, whose birth is reviled and who grows up untended and unloved, only to be wooed when 'at the age for love' (Ezekiel 16.8) by Yahweh.

Page 38, 'The sisters of famous men'. This poem mirrors, fairly precisely, the section in Virginia Woolf's *A Room of One's Own* on Shakespeare's sister (see earlier note).

Page 39, 'A litany for the young who dare to grow up different'. This litany celebrates a number of fictional children from contemporary film and one from fiction: Billy Elliot, the boy from a mining town who wants only to dance (*Billy Elliot*, written by Lee Hall and Daniel Dowdall, directed by Stephen Daldry and Tom Sheerin, starring Jamie Bell, Working Title Films and BBC Films, 2000); *Anne of Green Gables* (by Lucy Maude Montgomery, first published in 1908, also made into a TV series and a film), which I loved as a girl; Jamal Malik, the kid growing up in an Indian slum who becomes a millionaire (*Slumdog Millionaire*, written by Simon Beaufoy, directed by Danny Boyle, starring Dev Patel, Celedor Films and Film 4, 2008); and Paikea Apirana, the Maori girl who defies cultural norms by becoming the leader of her people (*Whale Rider*, based on the novel by Witi Ihimaera, directed by Niki Caro and starring Keisha Castle-Hughes, South Pacific Pictures, 2002).

Page 40, 'No oil painting'. The text from Isaiah 53, which forms one of the Suffering Servant songs that have inspired Christian understanding of Jesus throughout the centuries, speaks of the servant as one who 'had no form or majesty that we should look at him, nothing in his appearance that we should desire him'. Reflecting on this text, and the fact that artistic representations of Christ have by and large cast him as an ideal type representing masculine strength and beauty, I wanted to imagine a Christa who might be regarded as *un*attractive, ugly even, and certainly a disturbing character – one whom men, in particular, might not want to look at.

Page 41, 'Christa in the wilderness'. Apart from the biblical narratives of Christ in the wilderness, this poem was inspired by reading Belden C. Lane's powerful and moving exploration of desert spirituality, *The Solace of Fierce Landscapes* (New York: Oxford University Press, 1998), and the title phrase finds its way into the poem.

3 The table of women

Page 43. For discussion of women's presence at the Last Supper, see Dorothy A. Lee, 'Women Disciples at the Last Supper', in Judi Fisher and Janet Wood (eds), *A Place at the Table: Women at the Last Supper* (Melbourne: Joint Board of Christian Education, 1993). Lee surveys each of the Gospels in turn, and shows that there are a variety of traditions, not only as to whether women were present, but as to what kind of a meal it was (Passover or not), and that there is a confusing absence and presence of women throughout. Nevertheless, she suggests, 'Given the practice of Jesus' ministry, it is hard to imagine that, on the critical occasion of his final meal, the women (and other disciples outside the twelve) who faithfully followed him from Galilee would be excluded from table fellowship' (p. 82). However, as the status of the twelve apostles increased in the decades following, 'the importance of other disciples in the Last Supper (especially men) decreased' and began to disappear from some of the biblical texts.

Page 43. For feminist theological analysis of the Eucharist, see Susan A. Ross, *Extravagant Affections: A Feminist Sacramental Theology* (New York/ London: Continuum, 2001) and Marjorie Procter-Smith, *Praying with Our Eyes Open: Engendering Feminist Liturgical Prayer* (Nashville, TN: Abingdon, 1995), ch. 6. For feminist reflection on Maundy Thursday as such, see Teresa Berger, *Fragments of Real Presence: Liturgical Traditions in the Hands of Women* (New York: Crossroad, 2005), pp. 187–9, and for examples of feminist liturgies for Maundy Thursday, see Dorothea McEwan, Pat Pinsent, Ianthe Pratt and Veronica Seddon (eds), *Making Liturgy: Creating Rituals for Worship and Life* (Norwich: Canterbury Press, 2001), pp. 76–83; and Janet Morley, *All Desires Known*, 3rd edn (London: SPCK, 2005), pp. 66–8.

Page 44. The quotation from Anita Monro is in her essay ' "And Ain't I a Woman": The Phonetic Dramaturgy of Feeding the Family', p. 128.

Page 46, 'In memory of her'. This poem uses as a refrain the title of Elisabeth Schüssler Fiorenza's classic reconstruction of women's roles in the earliest Christian communities, *In Memory of Her: A Feminist Theological Reconstruction of Christian Origins* (London: SCM Press, 1983) – a title which Fiorenza herself, of course, based on the gospel text in Mark 14.9 in which Jesus tells the unnamed woman who anoints him that what she has done will be told 'in memory of her' wherever the gospel is proclaimed. Fiorenza was the first to point out the irony that 'wherever the gospel is proclaimed and the eucharist celebrated another story is told: the story of the apostle who betrayed Jesus. The name of the betrayer is remembered, but the name of the faithful disciple is forgotten because she was a woman' (p. xiii). As Fiorenza argues, 'as long as the stories and history of women in the beginnings of early Christianity are not theologically conceptualized as an integral part of the proclamation of the gospel, biblical texts and traditions formulated and codified by men will remain oppressive to women' (p. xv).

Page 47, 'The anointing'. This poem is dedicated to Ramona Kauth, who has been blessing me with the gift of massage, as well as her gentle and wise friendship, for many years.

Page 48, 'Christa gives a mud wrap'. This piece, and the collect 'Christa our healer' (page 149), were inspired by, and based directly on, a variety of experiences of therapeutic mud-pools in New Zealand, especially the unforgettable pools at Ngawha Spring, all eight of them (individually named – 'Lobster', 'Tranquillity', 'Cinnamon' and so on, each of a somewhat different colour, temperature and mineral content), which I enjoyed on a crisp, bright winter solstice day, and the unique experience of receiving a 'mud wrap' at the QE Health Centre on the edge of Lake Rotorua (Rotorua being the centre of all things thermal in the North Island, New Zealand).

Page 51, 'Her face'. This poem and others in the book ('Pavane pour une enfante défuncte' and 'Shekinah') were prompted by Melissa Raphael's extraordinary book, *The Female Face of God in Auschwitz: A Jewish Feminist Theology of the Holocaust* (London/New York: Routledge, 2003) – at once a meticulously researched, scholarly text, a harrowing account of women's experience in the death camps, an exquisitely written work of lyrical intensity, and an original, creative hypothesis suggesting that women's neglected experience in Auschwitz gestures towards the presence of a maternal God in the Holocaust beyond the death of the patriarchal God whom many Jewish theologians have no longer been able to postulate after the death camps. I have found this book one of the most moving and challenging I have ever read, especially as a Christian theologian, yet at the same time it has been for me revelation, an epiphany of the face and compassionate presence of Christa in a place where one might least (or most?) expect to find her. This particular poem reflects Raphael's detailed descriptions of the ways in which women in the camps sought to care for one another through mundane, bodily actions such as washing one another's faces and bodies, despite the lack of anything but unspeakably filthy water, or combing and stroking each other's hair – acts which Raphael reads as a kind of compulsive maternal care, beyond any hope of such care effecting any significant change in the women's circumstances or bodily state. It also picks up Raphael's meditation on the significance of the human face in Jewish theology – especially in the work of Emmanuel Levinas – as the site where the image of God is most intimately revealed *and* concealed. 'Where women in Auschwitz, each in God's image, turned (in whatever sense) to face the other, they refracted God's face or presence into the world from the light of their own. Compassion was transfigurative. When a woman saw or looked into the face of the suffering other (and that other's filthy, beaten, vacated face, was not easy to see and to look upon) the divine humanity of that face could be traced through the thick scale of its physical and spiritual profanation' (*Female Face of God*, pp. 7–8). The poem quotes freely from the text or alludes to Raphael's terms, images and dense theology. I am grateful to Melissa for her generous encouragement of my adaptation of her work in this way (through personal email and conversation).

Page 52, 'The table of women'. This poem is based on a description of eucharistic imagery in the catacombs highlighted by Rita Nakashima Brock and Rebecca Ann Parker in their book, *Saving Paradise: How Christianity Traded Love of This World for Crucifixion and Empire* (Boston: Beacon Press, 2008): 'In the Christian catacombs in Rome, images of the loaves and fish are frequent motifs. Large baskets of bread and platters of fish are set around a table with seven people enjoying the food. One delightful image in the Priscilla catacombs shows a table of women. In another, an inscription says the women call, "Bring it warm!"' (p. 30). This homely, life-affirming image struck me as a significant one, at the same time suggestive of women's centrality to the celebration of the Eucharist from earliest times, and subversive of theologies of the Eucharist which have centred on death and sacrifice. As Brock and Parker argue in their book, the earliest Christian imagery centred on the celebration of life, conceived as Paradise – a paradise on this earth which Christ had restored to believers by his life and his death.

Page 54, 'A litany for messy eaters'. This piece originally appeared (in a very slightly different form) in *The Edge of God: New Liturgical Texts and Contexts in Conversation*, ed. Stephen Burns, Michael N. Jagessar and

Nicola Slee (Peterborough: Epworth, 2008), as part of an essay co-written with Claire Carson, 'Brokenness, Love and Embrace: Eating Disorders and the Eucharist'. (Reproduced by permission of Epworth Press.) The refrain is, of course, taken from the eucharistic liturgy, a refrain that is often used at the fraction in Anglican churches. In the essay, we explore some of the ambivalence of food imagery for Christians with eating disorders (as well as others), and this litany attempts to acknowledge something of the differing, and conflictual, experiences and understandings Christians bring to the eucharistic table.

Page 56, 'At the table of Christa'. This poem originally appeared in *Presiding Like a Woman*, ed. Nicola Slee and Stephen Burns (London: SPCK, 2010), p. 178.

Page 57, 'Presiding like a woman'. This piece was also first published in *Presiding Like a Woman*, pp. 7–8, and was largely inspired by Stephen Burns' article, 'Presiding Like a Woman: Feminist Gestures for Christian Assembly', *Feminist Theology* 18 (2009), pp. 29–49.

Page 59, 'The agony'. In this piece, I'm trying to find a way of articulating the agonizing struggle that has been very real in my own journey, and which I have heard echoed in the stories of other women, to accept the cup, not so much of suffering and death (as in the narrative of Jesus' agony), as of that of *life*, power and vitality which, for some women, is more fearful than saying 'yes' to suffering and self-annihilation.

Page 63, 'The body of Christa'. This, and the following piece, draw very obviously – though not directly from any one source – on the work of ecofeminist writers and theologians who, for several decades now, have been exploring the connections between the oppression and suffering of women on the one hand, and the suffering of our endangered planet. The bodies of women and the body of the earth have been closely associated from the earliest days of Christian thinking, and their identification is part of a whole dualistic world-view which has separated earth from heaven, women from men, flesh from spirit, passion from rationality, and so on, elevating the latter over the former, and subjugating the former to the latter. Classic texts of ecofeminist theology include Catharine J. M. Halkes, *New Creation: Christian Feminism and the Renewal of the Earth* (London: SPCK, 1991); Sallie McFague, *The Body of God: An Ecological Theology* (London: SCM Press, 1993); Rosemary Radford Ruether, *Gaia and God: An Ecofeminist Theology of Earth Healing* (London: SCM Press, 1993); Rosemary Radford Ruether (ed.), *Women Healing Earth: Third World Women on Ecology, Feminism and Religion* (London: SCM Press, 1996); Ivone Gebara, *Longing for Running Water: Ecofeminism and Liberation* (Minneapolis, MN: Fortress Press, 1999); Sallie McFague, *Life Abundant* (Minneapolis, MN: Fortress Press, 2001) and Mary Grey, *Sacred Longings: Ecofeminist Theology and Globalization* (London: SCM Press, 2003).

Page 62, 'A litany for Passiontide'. This piece was written to serve as part of the Good Friday liturgy at St James, Piccadilly, 2010, where I was giving the addresses which focused on the Christa.

4 Christa crucified

Page 66. There is a considerable literature on feminist theological responses to the cross and the death of Jesus. For a basic summary overview, see my *Faith and Feminism: An Introduction to Christian Feminist Theology* (London: Darton, Longman and Todd, 2003), ch. 6. See also Natalie K. Watson, 'A Wider View or the Place where Love Is Possible: Feminist Theology, the Cross and Christian Tradition', in Natalie K. Watson and Stephen Burns (eds), *Exchanges of Grace: Essays in Honour of Ann Loades* (London: SCM Press, 2008), pp. 15–23. For fuller treatments, see (among many others) Mary Grey, *Redeeming the Dream* (London: SPCK, 1989), Colleen Carpenter Cullinan, *Redeeming the Story: Women, Suffering and Christ* (London: Continuum, 2004) and Barbara E. Reid, *Taking Up the Cross: New Testament Interpretations Through Latina and Feminist Eyes* (Minneapolis, MN: Fortress Press, 2007). For feminist discussions of the liturgical celebration of Good Friday, see Ann Patrick Ware, 'The Easter Vigil: A Theological and Liturgical Critique', in Marjorie Procter-Smith and Janet R. Walton (eds), *Women at Worship: Interpretations of North American Diversity* (Louisville, KY: Westminster/John Knox Press, 1993), pp. 83–106 and Teresa Berger, *Fragments of Real Presence: Liturgical Traditions in the Hands of Women* (New York: Crossroad, 2005), pp. 189–91. For examples of feminist liturgies of the cross and/or for Good Friday, see Janet Morley, *All Desires Known*, 3rd edn (London: SPCK, 2005), pp. 68–9; Miriam Therese Winter, *WomanWord: A Feminist Lectionary and Psalter, Women of the New Testament* (New York: Crossroad, 1990), pp. 135ff.; Barbara Cawthorne Crafton, 'The Seven Last Words of Christ', in Elizabeth Rankin Geitz, Marjorie A. Burke and Ann Smith (eds), *Women's Uncommon Prayers: Our Lives Revealed, Nurtured, Celebrated* (Harrisburg, PA: Morehouse, 2000), pp. 295–300; Susanna Gunner, 'Women-Cross', in Margaret Rose, Jenny Te Paa, Jeanne Person and Abagail Nelson (eds), *Lifting Women's Voices: Prayers to Change the World* (Norwich: Canterbury Press, 2009), pp. 184–8.

Page 72, 'Wrestling with the cross: journal extract'. The texts referred to are Marjorie Procter-Smith, *Praying with Our Eyes Open: Engendering Feminist Liturgical Prayer* (Nashville, TN: Abingdon, 1995) and Joanne Carlson Brown and Carole R. Bohn (eds), *Christianity, Patriarchy and Abuse: A Feminist Critique* (Boston: Pilgrim Press, 1989). The 2000 exhibition 'Seeing Salvation' was a hugely popular exhibition that drew crowds. See *The Image of Christ: The Catalogue of the Exhibition Seeing Salvation* (London: National Gallery Company, 2000).

Notes, sources and acknowledgements

Page 77, 'Confession for Good Friday'. This piece was written for the Good Friday liturgy at St James, Piccadilly, April 2010.

Page 79, 'Christa crucified'. This piece was a reflection on the proliferation and dominance of images of a crucified female form in contemporary art, but was provoked in particular by the disturbing sculpture, *Christine on the Cross* by James M. Murphy, which shows a naked woman pinned to an inverted crossbar, with legs, rather than arms, spreadeagled, in a pose that reveals her open vagina and may suggest 'shades of a pole-dancer with something come-hither in her jutting breasts; erect nipples and exposed vulva' (so Susannah Cornwall), as well as symbolizing male 'hostility toward women, with implications of submission, sexual humiliation and rape' (as expressed by the artist himself). See Julie Clague, 'The Christa: Symbolizing My Humanity and My Pain', *Feminist Theology* 14 (2005), pp. 83–108 and Susannah Cornwall, 'Ambiguous Bodies, Ambiguous Readings: Reflections on James M. Murphy's "Christine on the Cross"', in Zowie Davy et al. (eds), *Bound and Unbound: Interdisciplinary Approaches to Genders and Sexualities* (Newcastle: Cambridge Scholars Publishing, 2008), pp. 93–111.

Page 80, 'The concubine's communiqué'. Judges 19 tells the story of a concubine whose body is raped and abused by a group of men from Gibeah until she dies; her body is then cut into twelve pieces by her husband and sent 'through the length and breadth of Israel' (Judges 19.29) as a summons to revenge the outrage done against the Levite. This is one of four texts from Judges examined by Phyllis Trible in her classic *Texts of Terror: Literary-Feminist Readings of Biblical Narratives* (Philadelphia: Fortress Press, 1984), in which women are raped, abused, murdered and dismembered while the text shows little or no interest in their horrific suffering – texts which therefore pose particular challenges to feminists and indeed any contemporary reader seeking a liberating word from archaic, patriarchal Scriptures. This piece was written originally for a Bible study session I co-led with my colleague at Queen's, Lynnette Mullings, for the MA module, 'Reading the Bible Contextually and Inter-culturally', in which we explored feminist and womanist readings of Scripture and illustrated them by reference to this story. I am grateful to Lynnette for conversations we shared in preparing this session, and to other members of staff and students involved in the MA, for their stimulating responses to the text.

Page 82, 'A daughter's prayer of abandonment'. While not explicitly referring to any one scriptural text, this piece has a number of texts in view: perhaps most obviously, Jesus' cry of dereliction from the cross, 'My God, my God, why have you forsaken me?' (Mark 15.34); also the Good Friday reproaches, traditionally reproaches of God against God's faithless people, but reworked by some feminists as reproaches against God (see, for example, Marjorie Procter-Smith's 'mourning meal' in *Praying with Our Eyes Open*, pp. 137–8;

and the story of Jephthah's daughter in Judges 11, who is sacrificed by
her father in order to fulfil a vow to the Lord (ironically, the text voices
the father's lament against his daughter for 'breaking his heart' and bringing
calamity upon him (Judges 11.35), but no lament or reproach from the
daughter is uttered).

Page 83, 'A canticle for Passiontide'. This piece, based on a traditional Passiontide
canticle using Isaiah 63 (as found, for example, in 'A Song of the Lord's
Gracious Deeds' in *Common Worship: Daily Prayer*, London: Church House
Publishing, 2005, p. 588), engages feminist discussion of the symbolic
significance of blood, reflecting the irony that, while the blood of Jesus shed
in a violent death has been seen as salvific, women's menstrual and birth
blood have been regarded as taboo, ritually unclean. This piece identifies
the blood of the Messianic figure of Isaiah 63 with women's blood.

Page 84, 'Pavane pour une enfante défuncte'. The title refers to Ravel's haunting
solo piano piece. For the background in Melissa Raphael's work, see note
on 'Her face', p. 159.

Page 85, 'A prayer to Mother God'. This piece was prompted by Barbara E. Reid's
discussion of maternal imagery in Scripture and Christian tradition as
one source of alternative feminist models of redemption, in *Taking Up
the Cross*, ch. 5. In particular, I draw directly on the work of Jeannette
Rodríguez on the Virgin of Guadalupe in this prayer, quoted by Reid, in
which she speaks of the way in which the Virgin of Guadalupe reveals
something of the nature of God: 'God is the source of all life, maternal,
compassionate, and present, and protects the poor and the marginalized'
(*Our Lady of Guadalupe: Faith and Empowerment among Mexican-American
Women*, Austin, TX: University of Texas Press, 1994, p. 151).

Page 87, 'A litany to Christa our friend'. Like the prayer to Mother God on
pp. 85–6, this litany arose out of reflection on Barbara E. Reid's work in
Taking Up the Cross, particularly in ch. 1, where she rejects the idea that
understanding the death of Jesus as a sacrifice or atonement for sin is the
dominant New Testament model. Rather, she suggests, the Gospels describe
a Jesus who 'freely offers forgiveness for sin during his lifetime without
cultic sacrifice and without any reference to his death' (p. 46).
In particular, John's Gospel offers the model of Jesus as the friend who
voluntarily lays down his life for his friends out of love. Reid offers a
number of examples of biblical and contemporary women who, standing
in this tradition, give their lives willingly and freely out of deep love. Thus
this litany attempts to find a way of naming costly, sacrificial love that is
rooted in a fundamental life rather than death orientation (what Daly
would name 'biophiliac' as opposed to 'necrophiliac') and that does not
valorize violence. The biblical references are to the midwives in Exodus
1, the poor widow in Luke 21.1–4, the woman who anointed Jesus' feet

in Luke 7.37–50 (and parallels) and the Syro-Phoenician woman in Mark 7.24–30 (and Matthean parallel).

Page 93, 'Tree of life'. Lucy d'Souza-Krone's rendering of a female Christ in the form of a tree of life is the centre of a panel entitled *The Feminine Aspect of God*, which features images of the compassionate, luminous/glorious, wisdom and nurturing aspects of God, and can be found at <http://www. lucy-art.de/seite7.htm>. D'Souza-Krone's work features other symbols of the Christa, notably the centrepiece of her Lenten hunger-cloth featuring images of women in the Bible, which shows a woman kneading bread (from one of Jesus' parables of the kingdom), well-known in the UK as the cover image of the first edition of *Bread of Tomorrow*, a collection of prayers edited by Janet Morley (London: SPCK/Christian Aid, 1992) available at <http://www.hanna-strack-verlag.de/preis/preistraeger03.html>.

5 The feminist gap

Page 94. Two recent and significant reflections on Holy Saturday are Ian G. Wallis's *Holy Saturday Faith: Rediscovering the Legacy of Jesus* (London: SPCK, 2000) and Alan E. Lewis's *Between Cross and Resurrection: A Theology of Holy Saturday* (Grand Rapids, MI: Eerdmans, 2001).

Page 95. For details of my research into women's faith lives, see my *Women's Faith Development: Patterns and Processes* (Aldershot, Ashgate, 2004). See also my article 'Apophatic Faithing in Women's Spirituality', *British Journal of Theological Education* 11.2 (2001), pp. 23–7. The reference to William Bridges' 'neutral zone' is from his *Transitions: Making Sense of Life's Changes* (Reading, MA: Addison-Wesley, 1980).

Page 102, 'Lullaby'. This poem was, in some measure, a response to a small stone sculpture of a woman lying in a bath by Juginder Lamba, which formed one of the exhibits in a collection of his sculptures shown at the Water Hall, Birmingham, entitled 'Body and Soul', during 2008. For more about the sculptor, and examples of his work (though not this particular sculpture), see <http://www.juginderlamba.co.uk>, and *Juginder Lamba: Sculptures* (Eastbourne: Leaf and Stream, 2007).

Page 103, 'Wrapping the bones'. In March 2004, I attended a workshop at Woodbrooke Quaker Study Centre given by Marian Partington, sister of Lucy Partington, who was one of Fred and Rosemary West's victims. Lucy disappeared from a bus-stop in 1973, after visiting a friend, and it was only twenty years later that her body was discovered, along with the remains of other victims, at 25 Cromwell Street, Gloucester. In the work-shop, Marian Partington spoke about the importance of being able to handle, wrap and bury her sister's bones, some twenty years after her disappearance – something that made a huge impact on me, as well as others there. As part of the workshop, we were given opportunities to write and also to make Buddhist prayer flags – referred to in this poem. Marian Partington has written about her experience in 'You Would Have Been a Brilliant Aunt', *Guardian*, Wednesday 10 April 2002, online at <http://www.guardian.co.uk/lifeandstyle/2002/apr/10/familyandrelationships.features10>. See also Marian Partington, 'A Shining Silence', at <http://www.westernchanfellowship.org/a-shining-silence.html>.

Page 104, 'Green grave'. This poem was one of a sequence written for the Southwell Poetry Festival 2004, responding to various sites inside and outside Southwell Minster, and performed as part of a Remembrance Day tour of the Minster, shared with Rosie Miles and local historian Rowena Edlin-White (the poems all had some kind of focus on 'remembrance', broadly interpreted). This particular poem was prompted by a grave that was literally covered all over in ivy, so that no details could be read of the person buried there.

Page 106, 'Woman settling into her sabbatical'. An extract from my personal journal while on sabbatical at Vaughan Park Anglican Retreat Centre (<http://www.vaughanpark.org.nz>). The May Sarton poem referred to is 'On being given time', in *Selected Poems of May Sarton*, edited by Serena Sue Hilsinger and Lois Brynes (New York: W. W. Norton, 1978), p. 87. In fact, I'd misremembered the line, which is 'Even a year's not long, yet moments are'.

6 Christa rising

Page 110. The quotation is from Gillian Limb, Veronica Seddon and Mairin Valdez, *Death and Renewal of Creation: A Women's Approach to the Easter Experience* (London: Catholic Women's Network, 2002), p. 3.

Page 110. For feminist theological interpretations of resurrection, see the discussion in ch. 1 (pp. 24–7). For examples of feminist Easter liturgies, see Limb et al., *Death and Renewal of Creation*, pp. 20–3; Dorothea McEwan, Pat Pinsent, Ianthe Pratt and Veronica Seddon (eds), *Making Liturgy: Creating Rituals for Worship and Life* (Norwich: Canterbury Press, 2001), pp. 95–6; Teresa Berger, *Fragments of Real Presence: Liturgical Traditions in the Hands of Women* (New York: Crossroad, 2005), pp. 192–3; Janet Morley, *All Desires Known*, 3rd edn (London: SPCK, 2005), pp. 70–1; Miriam Therese Winter, *WomanWord: A Feminist Lectionary and Psalter, Women of the New Testament* (New York: Crossroad, 1990), pp. 156ff.; and Elizabeth Rankin Geitz, Marjorie A. Burke and Ann Smith (eds), *Women's Uncommon Prayers: Our Lives Revealed, Nurtured, Celebrated* (Harrisburg, PA: Morehouse, 2000), pp. 303ff.

Page 110. Joanna Collicutt McGrath's words are from her *Jesus and the Gospel Women* (London: SPCK, 2009), p. xiii.

Page 111. John Henson's fresh and daring translation of the New Testament is *Good as New: A Radical Retelling of the Scriptures* (Washington/Winchester: O Books, 2004).

Page 114, 'Litany of the women in search of a risen Christa'. The notion of 'natality' was developed by Grace Jantzen to call attention to the fact that human beings share in common our birth experience, the fact that we are all 'natals', and as a counter to the emphasis on mortality and death in Western philosophy (the obsession with 'necrophilia', as Mary Daly has it in *Beyond God the Father*, 2ⁿᵈ edn (London: Women's Press, 1986)). Jantzen herself was only able to begin to sketch out a comprehensive philosophy of religion based on the notion of natality and flourishing before her death in 2006. See her *Becoming Divine: Towards a Feminist Philosophy of Religion* (Manchester: University of Manchester Press, 1998). I am grateful to the Revd Jennie Hurd, who is currently conducting doctoral research into the pastoral applicability of Jantzen's notion of natality under my supervision, for creative conversations around this concept.

Page 115, 'Christa, at the door'. I became fascinated by the imagery of locked and opened doors in the Johannine narratives of the resurrection, where we find the disciples hiding in locked rooms 'for fear of the Jews' (John 20.19) and the risen Christ appearing miraculously through locked doors on a number of occasions (John 20.19, 26). This imagery is repeated in other places in the New Testament, for example, in Acts 12, where an angel unlocks the prison gates and releases Peter, and in a number of places in Revelation, notably 3.8, 20, where Christ is imaged as one knocking on the door of the believer's heart, seeking entry, and 4.1. Revelation 3.20 was, famously, the inspiration for Holman Hunt's painting of Christ as the Light of the World, in which Christ is depicted knocking on a door with no handle or key, suggestive of the way in which the Saviour can only have access to the one who opens from within. (There are numerous versions of this painting easily accessible online.)

Page 121, 'Christa of the red dress'. This poem is a celebration of, and an attempt to respond in words to, Emmanuel Garibay's wonderful image of Emmaus that adorns the cover of this book. Of all the images of a female Christ I have come across, this is probably my favourite, not only because of its joyous energy and a kind of naturalism about the very *ordinariness* of a female Christ figure, but also because it presents, almost uniquely among all the representations I have been able to find, a *collective* image of the Christa. I want to say that the Christa in this painting is not simply the central female figure, but is the whole group of engaged, enlivened companions. Garibay has painted several versions of this encounter. See <http://www.emmanuelgaribay.com> and <http://www.asianchristianart.org/galleries/resurrection/pages/Garibay.html>.

Page 122, 'The Maori Christa'. This poem first appeared in *New Zealand Books* 20.4 (Issue 92), Summer 2010, and is reprinted here by permission of the editors. It is one of a number of pieces on the Christa that were written during my sabbatical in New Zealand and that attempt to engage seriously (though recognizing my own status as an outsider and a very temporary visitor, a true Pakeha) with the landscape and history, the politics and culture(s) of the land and the peoples who inhabit the 'long white cloud'. For those who do not know New Zealand, the following notes may be helpful as background. The poem engages in a dialogue with James K. Baxter's well-known (to Kiwis, anyway!), iconic poem, 'The Maori Jesus', which can be found in his *Selected Poems* (ed. Paul Millar, Manchester: Carcanet, 2010), pp. 145–6, and is frequently anthologized – for example, in Robert Atwan, George Dardess and Peggy Rosenthal (eds), *Divine Inspiration: The Life of Jesus in World Poetry* (Oxford: Oxford University Press, 1998). The Karangahape Road is one of Auckland's best-known streets, vibrant and somewhat seedy in parts, boasting sex shops, bars, clubs, trendy 'niche' shops and cafes and so on. Cape Reinga (in Maori, Te Rerenga Wairua, the leaping place of the spirits) is the most accessible northern point of the Aupouri Peninsula, at the northernmost tip of the North Island, a place of spectacular beauty and particularly sacred to Maori as the place where the spirits of the dead begin their journey of return to the ancestors. The Waitangi Treaty Grounds, now a major museum and tourist site, is perhaps 'the single most symbolic place in New Zealand for Maori and Pakeha alike' (*The Rough Guide to New Zealand*, London: Rough Guide, 2008), where the notorious Treaty of Waitangi was signed in 1840 by Maori chiefs and the British governor, in which Maori conceded sovereignty to the British in return for British protection. There were two versions of the treaty, one in English and one in Maori, with somewhat different meanings, such that the Maori chiefs had a different understanding of what they were signing than the British. The treaty continues to be a source of tension between Maori and Pakeha. The poi is a traditional form of dance performed by Maori women, in which white balls of raupo (bulrush) attached to string are swung around in intricate and complex movements. Greenstone, or jade, is symbolic of the land for Maori and of great spiritual value. Paua is New Zealand's endemic species of abalone which, when polished, produces a gorgeous iridescent shell of blue, green, silver and purple. Maori crafts make use of the shell in jewellery and it is now very common in items made for the tourist trade. Rotorua is a major tourist site and the centre of thermal activity in the North Island. Te Papa is the Museum of New Zealand in Wellington, a modern purpose-built building opened in 1998 celebrating the history, cultures and traditions of Maori, Pakeha and Polynesian peoples. The Anglican Church of St Faith's sits on the edge of Lake Rotorua in the small Maori village of Ohinemutu, and features a stained-glass image of Christ as a Maori chief, swathed in Maori cloak and feathers. 'Kia ora' is the standard greeting used by Pakeha and Maori alike. 'Mana' is a Maori word indicating status, esteem, prestige and spiritual authority.

Page 124, 'Christa bathing'. This poem is another based on my New Zealand experience and is a second kind of, much more idealized, version of a Maori Christa. It reflects the Maori profound respect for land and living beings as manifestations of the sacred, symbolized in particular by the reverence Maori accord to greenstone (jade), which is the emblem of the land par excellence. Considered by the Maori a taonga (treasure), tools, weapons and ornaments were made of it, and passed down from generation to generation, revered as possessing its own sacred mana.

Page 126, 'Christa, crone'. This poem was inspired by Gillian Allnutt's sequence of Nantucket poems from her collection, *Nantucket and the Angel* (Newcastle: Bloodaxe, 1997). Nantucket is an alter ego of her older self, giving expression to a female symbolic concerned with age and ageing.

Page 127, 'Her hands'. Jake Lever has created an exquisite series of drawings and etchings of hands, representing angel hands, Christ's hands and Magi hands, among others. For reproductions of some of these see <http://www.leverarts.co.uk> and *Touching the Sacred*, by Chris Thorpe and Jake Lever (Norwich: Canterbury Press, 2010). I am fortunate to own one of the series of Jake's Christ hands, and this poem is a response to this image.

Page 128, 'Only the wounded'. I came across the Gregory of Nyssa reference to his sister Macrina in B. A. B. Patterson, 'Redeemed Bodies: Fullness of Life', in N. L. Eisland and D. E. Saliers (eds), *Human Disability and the Service of God* (Nashville, TN: Abingdon, 1998), where Pattison writes of Macrina, 'Her earthly embodiment would not be erased. It mattered in the resurrection and by inference he [Gregory] claimed her disabilities as not only acceptable but also signs of her body's and God's goodness' (p. 126).

Page 131, 'Shekinah'. For the background in Melissa Raphael's work, see note on 'Her face', p. 159. 'Shekinah', a grammatically feminine term found frequently in the Hebrew Scriptures to refer to the dwelling or presence of God, has been the subject of much reflection by feminist theologians, both Jewish and Christian. See, for example, Rachel Montagu, 'Shechinah' [*sic*], in Lisa Isherwood and Dorothea McEwan (eds), *An A to Z of Feminist Theology* (Sheffield: Sheffield Academic Press, 1996), pp. 215–16.

Page 132, 'A risen woman'. I wrote this poem on the original Noddfa Easter retreat and, in one sense, the whole of the rest of this book has flowed from this single poem. I want to dedicate it particularly to all the women who shared that Noddfa Easter.

7 The kin-dom of Christa

'Kin-dom of Christa'. The notion of the 'kin-dom', rather than 'kingdom' of God,
is in common currency among feminist theologians to speak of the radical,
alternative community, based on a discipleship of equals, which Jesus
inaugurated. See Verna Elias, 'From Kingdom to Kin-dom: Three Feminist
Interpretations of the Kingdom of God', unpublished MA dissertation,
2001, University of Manitoba, available at <http://www.collectionscanada.
gc.ca/obj/s4/f2/dsk3/ftp05/MQ62723.pdf>.

Page 134. The section quoted from my earlier book, *Easter Garden: A Sequence
of Readings on the Resurrection Hope* (London: Collins Fount, 1990), can
be found on pp. 146–8.

Page 136. The reference to the psalms at the end of the introduction to this
chapter is to Ps. 18.19.

Page 137, 'Christa on the loose'. This poem draws freely and extensively on Gerard
Manley Hopkins' amazing poem, 'The Windhover', to elicit something of
the freedom of the ascended Christa I am after. The title draws on Janice
Raymond's study of friendship, *A Passion for Friends: Toward a Philosophy
of Female Affection* (London: Women's Press, 1986), in which she explores
the notion of the 'loose woman' as the free, unfettered woman who cannot
be controlled by men, thus reclaiming the term in a positive sense from
its historically pejorative associations. 'I contend that the original loose
woman is the free woman – loose and free from bonds and bondage to
men. The loose woman is the unattached woman. And because she resisted
attachment to men, she became deprived not only of patriarchal protection
but of patriarchal repute' (*A Passion for Friends*, p. 64).

page 140, 'Loose women'. See comments above on 'Christa on the loose' for the
positive reclamation of the notion of 'loose women' by feminists such as
Raymond.

Page 142, 'A canticle in praise of large women'. Several sources of inspiration
lie behind this poem: I have long loved Maya Angelou's show-stopping
poem, 'Phenomenal Woman', one of the most magnificent celebrations of
abundant female flesh that could be imagined, and hearing her perform
at the Hay Festival a few years back was one of those experiences always
to be cherished. The poem appears on the web in numerous places, and
can also be found in her *Complete Collected Poems* (London: Virago, 1995),
pp. 130–1, although there is nothing to compare with hearing her performing
it. A number of CDs are available of her reading her poems, and her own
website has examples too. See <http://mayaangelou.com>. More recently,
Lisa Isherwood's *The Fat Jesus* (Darton, Longman and Todd, 2007) has
stimulated me to rethink the whole issue of size and cultural attitudes to
female bodies, and is an obvious influence on this poem and other pieces
in this section. Lisa herself is an inspiration to many women and, as

Professor of Feminist Theology at the University of Winchester, a leading promoter and supporter of feminist theology in the UK whose publications alone have massively extended the range and creativity of feminist theology in this country (see <http://www.winchester.ac.uk/aboutus/lifelonglearning/Theologicalpartnerships/peopleprofiles/Pages/LisaIsherwood.aspx>). I have known June Boyce-Tillman, now Professor of Applied Music at the University of Winchester (see <http://www.winchester.ac.uk/academicdepartments/PerformingArts/peopleprofiles/Pages/TheReverendProfessorJuneBoyce-Tillman.aspx>) for many years, since we were first involved in Women in Theology in the 1980s and sat on its publication committee together. Her creativity, not only in the field of church music but also in her theology and educational practice, has again been inspirational to many, and she has done much to bring women's musical traditions and gifts into the limelight. Her feminist-inspired hymns, songs and chants are a gift to the Church (see *A Rainbow to Heaven*, London: Stainer and Bell, 2006). Helen Dixon Cameron is a friend and colleague at Queen's; our friendship goes back to 1997, when I first came to Queen's, and was cemented when we did a year's jobshare in 1998–9. She is a fine pastoral theologian, with a particular passion for literature and theatre (as well as shoes!), and another indefatigable woman whose energies and commitments amaze and inspire me.

Page 144, 'Christa, listening'. The theme of listening is a major one, not only in pastoral theology generally, but in feminist and womanist pastoral and practical theology particularly (as also in other liberation theologies), exemplified in the work of many feminist and womanist practical theologians and researchers who make an intentional commitment to listen to the experience of women and girls (and other marginalized, previously silenced groups) in places often ignored by mainstream theology, paying particular attention to listening to the silences and to what is *not* said. The whole theme of listening and 'hearing to speech' has become axiomatic in feminist theology generally and such a commitment underlies my own attempt to listen to women's experiences of faith in *Women's Faith Development: Patterns and Processes* (Aldershot: Ashgate, 2004).

Page 145, 'Oblation'. This poem, as so many throughout my life, was both written at Malling Abbey, in Kent, and is a tribute to the life of the sisters there and to the spiritual sustenance and renewal I have received there over many years. 'Oblation' has a technical as well as more general sense (from the Latin *oblatio*, offering) of any solemn offering to God, in that it refers to the commitment made by lay oblates who, after a period of training and discernment, may make a particular commitment to the monastery and to the Rule of Benedict. Although I am not formally an oblate of the community, I do have a deep attachment to the abbey, and the Rule of Benedict has become an important resource in my own spiritual life.

Page 146, 'Becoming divine'. This poem takes its title from Grace Jantzen's book of that name: *Becoming Divine: Towards a Feminist Philosophy of Religion* (Manchester: University of Manchester Press, 1998), and refers freely to many ideas and terms in that book, and in other of Jantzen's writings – which, themselves, owe much to the work of other feminist philosophers, particularly Luce Irigaray, whose suggestive writings on female divine becoming have been generative for many theologians, partly through the work of Jantzen. Jantzen explores the whole notion of what it might mean for women to 'become divine' (an idea, of course, not new to Christian theology, and one which the Orthodox tradition has taken seriously in its theology of deification), to claim divinity within their own bodies and female subjectivity, to discover and utilize our own voices, finding a language and symbolic from the gaps and fissures in patriarchal language and culture, celebrating a religion of (female) flourishing and natality. Although Jantzen's death, in 2006, prevented her from completing her hugely ambitious 3-part project exploring and expanding her thesis for a religion based on natality rather than death (the first volume published as *Foundations of Violence: Death and the Displacement of Beauty, Vol. 1*, London: Routledge, 2004; the second as *Violence to Eternity: Death and the Displacement of Beauty, Vol. 2*, ed. Jeremy Carrette and Morny Joy, London: Routledge, 2008; the third, *A Place of Springs: Death and the Displacement of Beauty, Vol. 3*, ed. Jeremy Carrette and Morny Joy, London: Routledge, 2009), her work has been hugely creative for many theologians and philosophers, and others are now continuing to develop the trajectories of her writing. Elaine Graham's recent celebration and exposition of Jantzen's work, *Grace Jantzen: Redeeming the Present* (Aldershot: Ashgate, 2009) is a testimony to her impact on philosophy of religion, ethics and theology and explores major themes in her work.

Christa collects

These collects were written as a direct response to the suggestion of Stephen Burns that I include more collects in the book because, as he put it, 'collects can immediately and most easily be put to use in worship'. I dedicate these collects to Stephen, as one who has recognized and supported my own efforts not only to *think* theologically but to *pray* as a (feminist) theologian and to do theology out of the place of such prayer; and as one who, in his own writing and praying, has encouraged and enlarged my own.

Page 149, 'The kenosis of patriarchy'. The phrase 'kenosis of patriarchy' comes from Rosemary Radford Ruether, *Sexism and God-Talk* (London: SCM Press, 1983), p. 137, referring to the emptying out of patriarchy's oppressive powers.

Index of titles and first lines

Note: Titles of poems are in italics, first lines in roman.